A To Z:
Lord, Let It Define Me

Words of Wisdom, Motivation and Inspiration

LaTangela Fay Sherman

Copyright © 2017 LaTangela Sherman

All rights reserved.

ISBN-13- 978-0692922903
ISBN-10- 0692922903

DEDICATIONS

This book is dedicated to my loving and devoted mother,

Rhonda Fay Lafayette Sherman.

The sacrifices you have made for me did not go unnoticed.

I thank God for you daily.

In loving memory of my grandparents:

Reverend Jessie Lafayette, Sr.

and

Mrs. Olive Olivia Wright Lafayette

I thank God for blessing me with such amazing examples of humble servants of the Lord.

CONTENTS

Acknowledgments	i
A	3
B	21
C	44
D	59
E	75
F	81
G	87
H	91
I	101
J	108
K	111
L	117
M	125
N	131
O	133
P	136
Q	143
R	148
S	156
T	170

LaTangela Fay Sherman

U	173
V	185
W	202
X	209
Y	210
Z	212

ACKNOWLEDGMENTS

Thank you.

Thank you to my family, friends and community that has supported my vision and kept me inspired along the way.

I love you.

I-722 (4/30) = W.W.I.A.

ABILITY |ə'bilitē|

: talent that enables someone to achieve a great deal : a man of exceptional ability.
: power to perform

"He who is ABLE to visualize it is ABLE to conquer it." Within each and every being there is a God granted ABILITY. Some have the ABILITY to inspire those who may have lost their inspiration. Others may have the ABILITY to break down the courage of the most courageous. ABILITY is equivalent to power. Power as we will discuss throughout the book will play a major role in helping us find and define how we handle our individual ABILITIES. Each day brings about a new challenge presenting a new obstacle and another chance to approach the situation. Take a moment to identify some of your personal ABILITIES that enhance your everyday situations. The ABILITY to make the best of your work day; the ABILITY to deal with the intolerable task that cross your path as an obvious test of your faith, patience and endurance. How is your ABILITY to be optimistic and realize that each day consist of 24 hours and it is within your ABILITY to make the good = great and the not so good = tolerable? The day will go on as scheduled whether you are smiling or crying over the bumps and bruises life has tossed your way. It can be frustrating to see the potential in someone's ABILITY being over taken by their lack of effort or submission to the fear of the great heights they can soar by committing themselves to their inner greatness.

Make today the day you use your ABILITY to nurture the ABILITY of someone along the way, encouraging them to use their ABILITIES to make the world we live in a more compassionate place to raise a generation as we are ABLE to make a difference for the better.

Ezra 2:69
They gave after their ABILITY unto the treasure of the work threescore and one thousand dreams of gold, and five thousand pounds of silver, and one hundred priests' garments.

Nehemiah 5:8
And I said unto them, We after our ABILITY have redeemed our brethren the Jews, which were sold unto the heathen; and will ye even sell your brethren? or shall they be sold unto us? Then held they their peace, and found nothing to answer.

Ecclesiastes 9:11
I returned, and saw under the sun, that the race is not given to the swift, nor the battle to the strong, neither yet bread to the wise, nor yet riches to men of understanding, nor yet favour to men of skill; but time and chance happeneth to them all.

Matthew 25:15
And unto one he gave five talents, to another two, and to another one: to every man according to his several ability; and straightway took his journey.

2 Corinthians 8:3
For to their power, I bear record yea, and beyond their power they were willing of themselves;

2 Corinthians 8:11
Now therefore perform the doing of it: that as there was a readiness to will, so there may be a performance also out of that which ye have.

Exodus 10:5
And they shall cover the face of the earth, that one cannot be ABLE to see the earth: and they shall eat the residue of that which is escaped, which remaineth unto you from the hail, and shall eat every tree which groweth for you out of the field.

Exodus 18:21
Moreover, thou shalt provide out of all the people ABLE men, such as fear God, men of truth, hating covetousness; and place such over them, to be rulers of thousands, and rulers of hundreds, rulers of fifties, and rulers of tens:

Exodus 18:23
If thou shalt do this thing, and God command thee so, then thou shalt be ABLE to endure, and all this people shall also go to their place in peace.

Numbers 1:3
From twenty years old and upward, all that are ABLE to go forth to war in Israel: thou and Aaron shall number them by their armies.

Exodus 18:18
Thou wilt surely wear away, both thou, and this people that is with thee; for this thing is too heavy for thee; thou art not able to perform it thyself alone.

Genesis 15:5
And he brought him forth abroad, and said, Look now toward heaven, and tell the stars if thou be able to number them: and he said unto him, So shall thy seed be.

I Corinthians 3:2
I have fed you with milk, and not with meat: for hitherto ye were not able to bear it, neither yet now are ye able.

James 3:2
For in many things we offend all. If any man offend not in word, the same is a perfect man, and able to bridle the whole body.

Romans 4:21
And being fully persuaded that, what he had promised, he was able also to perform.

I Corinthians 10:13
There hath no temptation taken you but such as is common to man; but God is faithful, who will not suffer you to be tempted above that ye are able; but will with the temptation also make a way to escape, that ye may be able to bear it.

Matthew 3:9
And think not to say within yourselves, We have Abraham to our father: for I say unto you, that God is able of these stones to raise up children unto Abraham.

Matthew 10:28
And fear not them which kill the body, but are not able to kill the soul: but rather fear him which is able to destroy both soul and body in hell.

Romans 4:21
And being fully persuaded that, what he had promised, he was able also to perform.

2 Corinthians 9:8
And God is able to make all grace abound toward you; that ye, always having all sufficiency in all things, may abound to every good work.

Ephesians 3:20
Now unto him that is able to do exceedingly abundantly above all that we ask or think, accordingly to the power that worketh in us,

2 Timothy 1:12
For the which cause I also suffer these things: nevertheless I am not ashamed: for I know whom I have believed, and am persuaded that he is able to keep that which I have committed unto him against that day.

Hebrews 11:19
Accounting that God was able to raise him up, even from the dead; from whence also he received him in a figure.

Jude 1:24
Now unto him that is able to keep you from falling, and to present you faultless before the presence of his glory with exceeding joy,

Matthew 9: 28
And when he was come into the house, the blind men came to him: and Jesues saith unto them, Believe ye that I am able to do this? They said unto him, Yea, Lord.

ACCEPTANCE |AK'SEPTƏNS

: the action or process of being received as adequate or suitable, typically to be admitted into a group : you must wait for acceptance into the club.

ACCEPTANCE in life is one of the most subliminal issues that we deal with on a constant basis. Young to the young at heart all want to be ACCEPTED. To be ACCEPTED gives you the secure feeling of being loved, wanted or even a part of. From the first playground memories to just this morning we have felt comfort in being ACCEPTED one way or another. Used to your better judgment ACCEPTANCE can be healthy to a certain extent. The feeling of being left out, neglected or even denied has caused such a state of depression around the globe leaving rates from crime and even suicide at an all- time high. Sad to think not fitting into a so called in-crowd can help determine one's self worth.

It is important for us to learn to ACCEPT ourselves as the child of a loving God that has created us in HIS own image. Believing that ACCEPTANCE of yourself is a positive reinforcement and everything else is just lagniappe will allow a certain level of comfort in your own skin. Walk a path that only the brave dare to roam. There will never be a day that we will be ACCEPTED by all so live each day in a way that will be ACCEPTABLE in HIS sight.

Self -ACCEPTANCE gives you a stronger foundation of your purpose in life. Self- ACCEPTANCE is a vertebra in your backbone that helps you stand tall amongst adversities that may arise.

"We cannot complain about the things that we allow or ACCEPT" is an important statement to practice every day. It will serve as a reminder before we throw a pity party for others or ourselves for some of the controllable issues we deal with.

Exo 28:38
It will be on Aaron's forehead, and Aaron will bear the iniquity of the holy things, which the Israelites are to sanctify by all their holy gifts; it will always be on his forehead, for their acceptance before the Lord.

Lev 1:3
If his offering is a burnt offering from the herd he must present it as a flawless male; he must present it at the entrance of the Meeting Tent for its acceptance before the Lord.

Rom 11:15
For if their rejection is the reconciliation of the world, what will their acceptance be but life from the dead?

1Ti 1:15
This saying is trustworthy and deserves full acceptance: "Christ Jesus came into the world to save sinners" – and I am the worst of them!

ACCOUNTABILITY |ə͵kountəˈbilitē

: responsibility

there must be accountability for the expenditure of every public cent responsibility, liability, answerability.

ACCOUNTABILITY is the responsibility of acknowledging your circumstance due to your decision in the matter.
In the body of Christ, we are all sisters and brothers and belong one to another. By identifying who we are in the belief of Christianity, looking out one for another should become a make of our being. A list of the seven deadly sins that are the cause of a battered relationship with God holds pride as a leading cause.
It is an unbearable attribute in the sight of the Lord, which quickly fills the space where humility breaks down. With ever action comes a reaction and with every decision comes an outcome. Thoroughly thinking through issues is very critical in life as there are consequences we will face. There is no one that we can blame for the choices we make.
ACCOUNTABILITY = responsibility and we are held ACCOUNTABLE for our daily actions.
Being ACCOUNTABLE for the role we play in the scheme of life heightens our responsibility of the roads we travel along our journey.
ACCOUNTABILITY is a sure sign of maturity. In our church we are held ACCOUNTABLE for spreading the gospel and leading the soul sick to our heavenly Father. On our jobs we are held ACCOUNTABLE for the tasks we are expected to perform.

In our homes we are held ACCOUNTABLE to maintain the daily functions to keep things in order. In our society we are held ACCOUNTABLE to act as suitable citizens. ACCOUNTABILITY brings a sense of expectation from each individual. Are you willing to be held ACCOUNTABLE for your decisions? Think twice before reacting in a harsh manor. Seek guidance from wise counsel while making choices you are willing to be held ACCOUNTABLE for.

Job 33:13
Why dost thou strive against him? For he giveth not account of any of his matters.

Deu 21:8
Do not blame your people Israel whom you redeemed, O Lord, and do not hold them accountable for the bloodshed of an innocent person." Then atonement will be made for the bloodshed.

Deu 23:21
When you make a vow to the Lord your God you must not delay in fulfilling it, for otherwise he will surely hold you accountable as a sinner.

Psa 10:4
The wicked man is so arrogant he always thinks, "God won't hold me accountable; he doesn't care."

Psa 10:13
Why does the wicked man reject God? He says to himself, "You will not hold me accountable."

Psa 10:15
Break the arm of the wicked and evil man! Hold him accountable for his wicked deeds, which he thought you would not discover.

Psa 69:27
Hold them accountable for all their sins! Do not vindicate them!

Psa 79:8
Do not hold us accountable for the sins of earlier generations! Quickly send your compassion our way, for we are in serious trouble!

Eze 3:18
When I say to the wicked, "You will certainly die," and you do not warn him – you do not speak out to warn the wicked to turn from his wicked deed and wicked lifestyle so that he may live – that wicked person will die for his iniquity, but I will hold you accountable for his death.

Eze 3:20
"When a righteous person turns from his righteousness and commits iniquity, and I set an obstacle 1 before him, he will die. If you have not warned him, he will die for his sin. The righteous deeds he performed will not be considered, but I will hold you accountable for his death.

Eze 7:3
The end is now upon you, and I will release my anger against you; I will judge you according to your behavior, I will hold you accountable for all your abominable practices.

Dan 6:2
Over them would be three supervisors, one of whom was Daniel. These satraps were accountable to them, so that the king's interests might not incur damage.

Hos 12:14
But Ephraim bitterly provoked him to anger; so he will hold him accountable for the blood he has shed, his Lord will repay him for the contempt he has shown.

Luk 11:50
so that this generation may be held accountable for the blood of all the prophets that has been shed since the beginning of the world,

Rom 3:19
Now we know that whatever the law says, it says to those who are under the law, so that every mouth may be silenced and the whole world may be held accountable to God.

2Ti 4:16
At my first defense no one appeared in my support; instead they all deserted me — may they not be held accountable for it.

ALONE |ə'lōn|

: having no one else present; on one's own : [as predic. adj.] she was alone that evening | [as adv.] he lives alone.

Being ALONE is not always thought of as glamorous or appealing as being the socialite of the town. But being ALONE lays a true foundation as of who you really are. The moment of self-worth. A time to explore your thoughts of life, goals and even obstacles that may arise while tackling daily issues. It's only ALONE in the quiet of the day that you are able to connect with that small still voice that gives confirmation on things you have spent numerous hours pondering. It's during those ALONE moments that visions are birthed and dreams are etched from the soul. Don't fret being ALONE thinking it's not the cool thing to do or look at yourself as an outsider because you aren't surrounded by family and friends 24-7 of each day. It is okay to allow yourself some ALONE time to nurture your spiritual growth. It is during my ALONE time I find the peace to sit still and focus on sharing words of encouragement to you.

True enough there are things that you have to complete today, but I challenge you to make time for yourself. Ignore the hustle and bustle of the world and spend some time ALONE to meditate and rejuvenate.

Exo 14:12

Isn't this what we told you in Egypt, 'Leave us alone so that we can serve the Egyptians, because it is better for us to serve the Egyptians than to die in the desert!'

Exo 22:20
"Whoever sacrifices to a god other than the Lord alone must be utterly destroyed.

Exo 23:11
But in the seventh year you must let it lie fallow and leave it alone so that the poor of your people may eat, and what they leave any animal in the field may eat; you must do likewise with your vineyard and your olive grove.

Exo 32:10
So now, leave me alone so that my anger can burn against them and I can destroy them, and I will make from you a great nation."

Num 11:14
I am not able to bear this entire people alone, because it is too heavy for me!

Num 23:9
For from the top of the rocks I see them; from the hills I watch them. Indeed, a nation that lives alone, and it will not be reckoned among the nations.

Deu 1:12
But how can I alone bear up under the burden of your hardship and strife?

Deu 4:35
You have been taught that the Lord alone is God — there is no other besides him.

Deu 8:3
So he humbled you by making you hungry and then feeding you with unfamiliar manna. He did this to teach you that humankind cannot live by bread alone, but also by everything that comes from the Lord's mouth.

Deu 16:20
You must pursue justice alone so that you may live and inherit the land the Lord your God is giving you.

Deu 18:2
They will have no inheritance in the midst of their fellow Israelites; the Lord alone is their inheritance, just as he had told them.

Deu 32:12
The Lord alone was guiding him, no foreign god was with him.

Jos 1:5
No one will be able to resist you all the days of your life. As I was with Moses, so I will be with you. I will not abandon you or leave you alone.

1Sa 11:3
The elders of Jabesh said to him, "Leave us alone for seven days so that we can send messengers throughout the territory of Israel. If there is no one who can deliver us, we will come out voluntarily to you."

1Ki 3:18
Then three days after I had my baby, this woman also had a baby. We were alone; there was no one else in the house except the two of us.

Job 1:16

While this one was still speaking, another messenger arrived and said, "The fire of God has fallen from heaven and has burned up the sheep and the servants — it has consumed them! And I — only I alone — escaped to tell you!"

Psa 62:2

He alone is my protector and deliverer. He is my refuge; I will not be upended.

Psa 62:5

Patiently wait for God alone, my soul! For he is the one who gives me confidence.

ATTITUDE | ˈatiˌt(y)oōd |

: a settled way of thinking or feeling about someone or something, typically one that is reflected in a person's behavior

She took a tough attitude toward other people's indulgences.
Being competitive is an attitude of mind.

ATTITUDE in life and towards life plays a major role as of how you allow things to work in your favor. With a loving spirit and a kind ATTITUDE you can determine your altitude of great heights.
Not often will you find a multitude willing to tolerate someone that is always on the defensive side of a conversation. It's far too difficult to find a common ground and get things resolved creating a great deal of controversy. Remember throughout your journey of life, your ATTITUDE will be one of the most memorable attributes you possess. Answer questions in a firm yet polite manner. Avoid being quick tempered with a combative rebuttal. Having a pleasant ATTITUDE will carve more notches in the road of success than a lot of other business tactics will. It is stated in Philippians 2:5 that " You should have the same ATTITUDE toward one another that Christ Jesus had".
In these days and times it seems to be a lot easier said than done.
The truth of the matter is, it was not any easier then, than now. Those were the characteristics that made Christ the example.

"He who controls your mind controls you." A simple phrase with truth beyond compare. The world we live in today is in shambles. The education of our children is suffering, health tolls are worse than the generation before and the economic frustration spreads like wildfire. Facing the rash outcome of the situations at hand may be a difficult pill to swallow. But where do we begin to tackle the issues head on and begin to make them better? The children are our future. Just as it took a village to raise a child in my mother's generation and her mother's generation the fact still remains the same.

Our ATTITUDE must reflect that of COMPASSION . It is a must that we care enough for the children of this generation to become involved in their lives.

The wonders that can flourish from becoming an influential role model that they can see is priceless. Let the children of today grasp the same ATTITUDE of love that nurtured the great leaders. Inspire the children to have a winning ATTITUDE. An ATTITUDE of change.

Speak the power of love, encouragement and determination into their lives.

I Ch 28:9

"And you, Solomon my son, obey the God of your father and serve him with a submissive attitude and a willing spirit, for the Lord examines all minds and understands every motive of one's thoughts. If you seek him, he will let you find him, but if you abandon him, he will reject you permanently.

2 Ch 32:25

But Hezekiah was ungrateful; he had a proud attitude, provoking God to be angry at him, as well as Judah and Jerusalem.

Psa 101:5
I will destroy anyone who slanders his neighbor in secret. I will not tolerate anyone who has a cocky demeanor and an arrogant attitude.

Psa 106:43
Many times he delivered them, but they had a rebellious attitude, and degraded themselves by their sin.

Isa 1:19
If you have a willing attitude and obey, then you will again eat the good crops of the land.

Phil 2:5
You should have the same attitude toward one another that Christ Jesus had

BALANCE | ˈbaləns |

: an even distribution of weight enabling someone or something to remain upright and steady

: Slipping in the mud but keeping their balance. She lost her balance

You may find yourself barged down with a million and one things to do on a daily basis. Taking care of the family, handling tasks on the job, working or attempting to find a second job, running errands, the minor chores and with everything else that makes the top thousand on your to-do list it seems nearly impossible to fit it all into your day and even more difficult for you to focus on self.

The lack of completion leads us to believe; Only if we had the limbs of an octopus or an extra three hours in a day, I would be able to BALANCE things a little better. That sounds good but the truth of the matter is if we had the limbs of an octopus and three extra hours in a day, it would only allow us more time to juggle more tasks.

It is important that we learn to manage our time wisely and BALANCE things in our lives. To my knowledge the magic formula to getting it done has not been released, but I'm willing to say the key to the equation is keeping God first and asking Him for guidance to lead you in the right direction. BALANCING a healthy relationship with God will clear your mind and reveal things that you may have not seen clearly without Him.

Coming to the realization that the things we placed first may actually fall lower on the totem pole may be an eye opening experience that will remove distractions and get you closer to achieving your goals. Often we clutter our lives with wants over needs.

And after committing so much time to one over the other it tends to make reorganizing a harder task than anticipated. This will require a lot of soul searching, honesty and sacrificing. Make sure that you are willing to put the right foot forward towards your journey before taking the first step. Having the blue print and standing still is worse than taking three steps back.
Take it in stride and BALANCE your scales.

Today I recommend you placing God first on your to-do list and watch the method of BALANCING your days become a lot less hectic as you will understand what should always come first on your agenda. BALANCE your focus.

BEGINNING | bi'gini ng

: the point in time or space at which something starts

From every finish line or fairy tale ending there is always reference to a starting point. The success stories of life often come from a humble BEGINNING. A point when your heart desires seem to be at an unreachable destination. It's at the BEGINNING where visions are born and actions are implemented. Quite often you hear people say that they are looking for a new BEGINNING. Looking for another chance to take life by the horns and use the past bumps and bruises to help them along another path. Reflecting on your life, where is your BEGINNING? The moment you knew you were walking in the steps of your purpose. Have you identified your BEGINNING? Every day is a day of thanksgiving and should BEGIN with a prayerful tone setting the pace of unspeakable joy promised by the King.

BEGIN holding yourself accountable for your actions. BEGIN to understand that every choice and decision you make is an earmarked seed sewn towards the harvest you plan to till in due season. Once you BEGIN to speak things into existence BEGIN to position yourself into a zone where you are able to focus.

Pace yourself and BEGIN doing self-evaluations.

BEGIN with a short term goal and diligently work towards accomplishing them and BEGIN to see your dreams become your reality.

Gen 1:1
In the beginning God created the heavens and the earth.

Gen 13:3
And he journeyed from place to place from the Negev as far as Bethel. He returned to the place where he had pitched his tent at the beginning, between Bethel and Ai.

Gen 43:33
They sat before him, arranged by order of birth, beginning with the firstborn and ending with the youngest. The men looked at each other in astonishment.

Gen 49:3
Reuben, you are my firstborn, my might and the beginning of my strength, outstanding in dignity, outstanding in power.

Exo 12:2
"This month is to be your beginning of months; it will be your first month of the year.

Num 16:47
So Aaron did as Moses commanded and ran into the middle of the assembly, where the plague was just beginning among the people. So he placed incense on the coals and made atonement for the people.

Deu 11:12
a land the Lord your God looks after. He is constantly attentive to it from the beginning to the end of the year.

Rut 1:22
So Naomi returned, accompanied by her Moabite daughter-in-law Ruth, who came back with her from the region of Moab. (Now they arrived in Bethlehem at the beginning of the barley harvest.)

2Sa 7:10
I will establish a place for my people Israel and settle them there; they will live there and not be disturbed anymore. Violent men will not oppress them again, as they did in the beginning

2Ki 13:20
Elisha died and was buried. Moabite raiding parties invaded the land at the beginning of the year.

1Ch 17:9
I will establish a place for my people Israel and settle them there; they will live there and not be disturbed anymore. Violent men will not oppress them again, as they did in the beginning

2Ch 17:3
The Lord was with Jehoshaphat because he followed in his ancestor David's footsteps at the beginning of his reign. He did not seek the Baals,

Ezr 4:6
At the beginning of the reign of Ahasuerus they filed an accusation against the inhabitants of Judah and Jerusalem.

Job 8:7
Your beginning will seem so small, since your future will flourish.

BEHAVIOR |bi'hāvyər
: the way in which one acts or conducts oneself

From a child we are expected to be on our best BEHAVIOR. When we were sent to school or went to visit friends for weekend sleepovers, our parents told us to be on our best BEHAVIOR and not to cause any problems. As adults we go to work and are expected to BEHAVE within a code of conduct. There are a lot of things in life that are out of our control. Circumstances that bring about uncomfortable situations that may apply pressure to our day to day operations. Issues that may cause us to BEHAVE out of the pattern we would normally choose. When we decide to counteract with negativity and display a level of ignorance, we voluntarily lose the battle by subsiding to the lack of self-control we display. Our BEHAVIOR screams volumes.
For many, seeing is believing.
Saying one thing and BAHAVING the opposite leaves room for doubt. It starts the chain reaction of what may be recognized as that of a shyster, labeling you as a person who carries along being petty or unable to stand your ground with a level head when the waves begin to rock the boat. During turmoil, we tend to tense up and lose direction of the path set before us. Our faith and level of trust in our relationship with God is put to the test. Is your BEHVIOR towards God different during the difficult times than those of overflow?
Do you find it easier to praise in the reign of abundance than the rain of your future testimony? We should pattern ourselves after the example Jesus set as He awoke amidst a storm and spoke to the winds and waves demanding them to "Peace... be still."

Although the currents were high and all those around Him were in a frantic state, He remained steadfast in knowing that God was still the same God that had His back and stood true to His word.

When we leave the comfort zone of family, friends or peers that may hold us to certain levels of expectancy, we may tend to BEHAVE differently. The thought of being free from the restraints of what we know is expected of us offers room to stray from what we know is the proper conduct. Our BEHAVIOR is an extension of our personality, which will go further and faster than we will in the physical. That's why it is important to be of good character and BEHAVE accordingly at all times. Live up to a reputation that you will not have to defend but extend.

Gal. 5:22-23
But the fruit of the Spirit is love, joy, peace, forbearance, kindness, goodness, faithfulness, gentleness and self-control. Against such things there is no law.

Titus 2:12
It teaches us to say "No" to ungodliness and worldly passions, and to live self-controlled, upright and godly lives in this present age,

Colossians 3:5
Put to death, therefore, whatever belongs to your earthly nature: sexual immorality, impurity, lust, evil desires and greed, which is idolatry.

1 Corinthians 6:9
Or do you not know that wrongdoers will not inherit the kingdom of God? Do not be deceived: Neither the sexually immoral nor idolaters nor adulterers nor men who have sex with men

Romans 3:23
For all have sinned and fall short of the glory of God.

Leviticus 18:22
Do not have sexual relations with a man as one does with a woman; that is detestable.

Ephesians 4:14-15
Then we will no longer be infants, tossed back and forth by the waves, and blown here and there by every wind of teaching and by the cunning and craftiness of people in their deceitful scheming.
15 Instead, speaking the truth in love, we will grow to become in every respect the mature body of him who is the head, that is, Christ.

BETRAY |bi'trā|
be disloyal to :

To BETRAY or defy someone is a form of disrespect that is hard to overlook.
I have come to the realization that it is usually those closest to you that hurt you the worse. A brutal reality but it is what it is.
At some point and time trust was a factor and you felt comfortable enough to reveal information that was sacred and maybe even confidential. Something that was to be stored in a secure place and held within. To discover your well-being may not have been in the interest of the one you trusted can leave a bitter taste behind.
It builds hostility towards that individual and maybe even towards yourself for not using better judgment as of who you placed in your circle. All relationships are affected by BETRAYAL.
Marriage success rates are lower than ever while the divorce rates are soaring higher than eagles. Walls are built and BETRAYAL is nothing new or uncommon. Think how Jesus must have felt when Judas BETRAYED him not once but three times to His face.
It can be utilized as a form gratification or self-greed. Some may use the art of BETRAYAL by using your information to expose you in an uncomfortable position and shun you from the graces you are accustomed to in an attempt to tarnish your reputation. There truly aren't any good explanations or justifications why people find the need to execute BETRAYAL other than continuing with the dog eat dog mentality cycle.
To know how it feels to be BETRAYED we should make a conscious effort to do right by one another and master the art of not BETRAYING anyone.

1Ch 12:17

David went out to meet them and said, "If you come to me in peace and want to help me, then I will make an alliance with you. But if you come to betray me to my enemies when I have not harmed you, may the God of our ancestors take notice and judge!"

Isa 16:3

"Bring a plan, make a decision! Provide some shade in the middle of the day! Hide the fugitives! Do not betray the one who tries to escape!

Hab 2:5

Indeed, wine will betray the proud, restless man! His appetite is as big as Sheol's; like death, he is never satisfied. He gathers all the nations; he seizes all peoples.

Mal 2:10

Do we not all have one father? Did not one God create us? Why do we betray one another, in this way making light of the covenant of our ancestors?

Mat 24:10

Then many will be led into sin, and they will betray one another and hate one another.

Mat 26:15

and said, "What will you give me to betray him into your hands?" So they set out thirty silver coins for him.

Mat 26:16

From that time on, Judas began looking for an opportunity to betray him.

Mat 26:21
And while they were eating he said, "I tell you the truth, one of you will betray me."

Mat 26:23
He answered, "The one who has dipped his hand into the bowl with me will betray me.

Mat 26:25
Then Judas, the one who would betray him, said, "Surely not I, Rabbi?" Jesus replied, "You have said it yourself."

Mar 14:10
Then Judas Iscariot, one of the twelve, went to the chief priests to betray Jesus into their hands.

Mar 14:11
When they heard this, they were delighted and promised to give him money. So Judas began looking for an opportunity to betray him.

Mar 14:18
While they were at the table eating, Jesus said, "I tell you the truth, one of you eating with me will betray me."

Luk 22:4
He went away and discussed with the chief priests and officers of the temple guard how he might betray Jesus, handing him over to them.

Luk 22:6
So Judas agreed and began looking for an opportunity to betray Jesus when no crowd was present.

Luk 22:48
But Jesus said to him, "Judas, would you betray the Son of Man with a kiss?"

Joh 6:64
But there are some of you who do not believe." (For Jesus had already known from the beginning who those were who did not believe, and who it was who would betray him.)

Joh 6:71
(Now he said this about Judas son of Simon Iscariot, for Judas, one of the twelve, was going to betray him.)

Joh 12:4
But Judas Iscariot, one of his disciples (the one who was going to betray him) said,

Joh 13:2
The evening meal 1 was in progress, and the devil had already put into the heart of Judas Iscariot, Simon's son, that he should betray Jesus.

BODY | ˈbädē |

1 the physical structure of a person or an animal, including the bones, flesh, and organs : it's important to keep your body in good condition

Our body is generally thought of as the physical structure of bones, flesh and organs. A uniquely and wonderfully construction piece of machinery that performs to the way you keep it maintained.

From what you put in it to what you put on it the body is a canvas.

It is our temple. As Christians it is important for us to be spiritually in shape. But let's not remove the importance of keeping our bodies in physically good shape as well. Being spiritually ready and not having the emotional or physical energy to perform the task is a frustration that becomes stumbling blocks along the way.

Are you getting the proper nutrients and rest your body needs in able to function properly? Without it our immune systems become weaker, and we are more vulnerable to illness.

With a lack of rest you are physically unprepared to perform at your best. With so many things to do in what seems to be such little time we tend to neglect our physical needs of designating time to work out and rest.

Let today be the day you decide to take better care of your BODY. From the foods you eat to the clothes you wear. Make more of a conscious effort that your BODY is a temple.

There's no need to wait for the beginning of a new year for a resolution. Start taking better care of yourself today.

Mind, BODY and soul.

Matthew 1:20
But as he considered these things, behold, an angel of the Lord appeared to him in a dream, saying, "Joseph, son of David, do not fear to take Mary as your wife, for that which is conceived in her is from the Holy Spirit.

Matthew 5:29
If your right eye causes you to sin, tear it out and throw it away. For it is better that you lose one of your members than that your whole body be thrown into hell.

Matthew 5:30
And if your right hand causes you to sin, cut it off and throw it away. For it is better that you lose one of your members than that your whole body go into hell.

Matthew 6:22
"The eye is the lamp of the body. So, if your eye is healthy, your whole body will be full of light,

Matthew 6:23
but if your eye is bad, your whole body will be full of darkness. If then the light in you is darkness, how great is the darkness!

Matthew 6:25
"Therefore I tell you, do not be anxious about your life, what you will eat or what you will drink, nor about your body, what you will put on. Is not life more than food, and the body more than clothing?

Matthew 8:6

The officer said, "Lord, my servant is at home in bed. He ·can't move his body [is paralyzed] and ·is in much pain [suffering terribly]."

BOLD |bōld|

: (of a person, action, or idea) showing an ability to take risks; confident and courageous : a bold attempt to solve the crisis | he was the only one bold enough to air his dislike.

For God has not given us the spirit of fear we should be BOLD in the actions we take with a clear conscience. The world is ruled through the BOLD actions of someone who decides not to blend in. To stand on what you believe and taking the risk that the next person may have been too shaken to attempt.

Being BOLD is being able to lean on what you believe and not depend on the opinion of others to determine your path.

There are consequences and repercussions that come along with each and every decision to be made. If there is a goal you have set to accomplish "No should NOt be an option", especially if it is used to acquire a positive outcome for yourself and those around you. It is never too late to pick up the pieces and begin from where you are.

Fear is amongst the strong holds that will prevent us from accomplishments. Often you will hear the phrase "a closed mouth don't get fed" and it is so true. Where there is someone too conquered by a lack of confidence there are twenty others who are BOLD enough to take the challenge head on. Where do you stand?

2Ch 23:1
In the seventh year Jehoiada made a bold move. He made a pact with the officers of the units of hundreds: Azariah son of Jehoram, Ishmael son of Jehochanan, Azariah son of Obed, Maaseiah son of Adaiah, and Elishaphat son of Zikri.

Psa 138:3
When I cried out for help, you answered me. You made me bold and energized me.

Pro 7:13
So she grabbed him and kissed him, and with a bold expression she said to him,

Eze 16:30
How sick is your heart, declares the sovereign Lord, when you perform all of these acts, the deeds of a bold prostitute.

Rom 10:20
And Isaiah is even bold enough to say, "I was found by those who did not seek me; I became well known to those who did not ask for me."

2Co 10:2
now I ask that when I am present I may not have to be bold with the confidence that (I expect) I will dare to use against some who consider us to be behaving according to human standards.

BOTTOM | ˈbätəm |
: the lowest point or part
: the part on which a thing rests; the underside

When we think of where we want to be in life the BOTTOM is not usually top three on our list.
The BOTTOM is not always the location discussed in victorious conversations.
Homes are built from the BOTTOM up. When there is an issue that brings about confusion you must get to the BOTTOM of things to find a resolution.
The top of the mountain isn't necessarily where the warrior found strength or inspiration, but it is at the BOTTOM of it where they skillfully crafted a route to climb it and relocated to another level.
Climbing to a higher height is impossible to do if you do not have a foundation to rise from. What is there to do if you feel as if you are at the top of your game and appear to be on the BOTTOM of the rankings? Stop and start over. Regroup, re-evaluate and revamp.
The realization that everyday won't be amongst your best is the first step of understanding that with each day comes a new BEGINNING; an outlet to stop, regroup and start over. Looking towards a higher level from the BOTTOM line is the encouragement to keep you pushing on.

Daniel 6:24
And the king commanded, and they brought those men which had accused Daniel, and they cast them to the den of lions, them, their children, and their wives; and the lions had the mastery of them, and brake all their bones in pieces or ever they came at the bottom of the den.

Matthew 27:51
And, behold, the vail of the temple was rent in twain from the top to bottom; and the earth did quake, and the rocks rent;

Mark 15:38
And the vail of the temple was rent in twain from the top to the bottom.

Revelation 9:1-2
And the fifth angel sounded, and I saw a star fall from heaven unto the earth; and to him was given the key of the bottomless pit.
And he opened the bottomless pit; and there arose a smoke out of the pit, as the smoke of a great furnace; and the sun and the air were darkened by reason of the smoke of the pit.

BATTLE | ˈbatl |

a sustained fight between large, organized armed forces :
he died in battle.
• a lengthy and difficult conflict or struggle

"The BATTLE is not yours, it's the Lords". We hear the phrase and even sing the song. But when conflicts arise and you feel your back pressed against the wall, how do you handle the BATTLE? Every BATTLE won't come in the form of which you may expect. While you may be looking for smoke signals to alert you of fire, the BATTLE may sound off as an explosion and cause a frantic state of panic. My BATTLE may not be the same as your BATTLE, but it's a fact that everyone is a target at one point or another. The enemy will attack. How prepared are you for the sneak attack of the enemy? Spiritual warfare happens every day, all day. The BATTLE field is only level as you make it. Different paths presents new CHALLENGES.

Jeremiah 50:22
A sound of battle is in the land, and of great destruction.

Judges 8:13
And Gideon the son of Joash returned from battle before the sun was up,

1 Samuel 17:21
For Israel and the Philistines had put the battle in array, army against army.

2 Samuel 18:6
So the people went out into the field against Israel: and the battle was in the wood of Ephraim;

1 Chronicles 26:27
Out of the spoils won in battles did they dedicate to maintain the house of the Lord.

Job 38:23
which I have reserved against the time of trouble, against the day of battle and war?

Psalm 76:3
There brake he the arrows of the bow, the shield, and the sword, and the battle. Selah.

Proverbs 21:31
The horse is prepared against the day of battle: but safety is of the Lord.

Jeremiah 46:3
Order ye the buckler and shield, and draw near to battle.

Numbers 31:14
And Moses was wroth with the officers of the host, with the captains over thousands, and captains over hundreds, which came from the battle.

Joshua 4:13
about forty thousand prepared for war passed over before the Lord unto battle, to the plains of Jericho.

1 Samuel 14:23
So the Lord saved Israel that day: and the battle passed over unto Beth-aven.

1 Samuel 31:3
And the battle went sore against Saul, and the archers hit him; and he was sore wounded of the archers.

2 Samuel 2:17
And there was a very sore battle that day; and Abner was beaten, and the men of Israel, before the servants of David.

2 Samuel 3:30
So Joab and Abishai his brother slew Abner, because he had slain their brother Asahel at Gibeon in the battle.

2 Samuel 10:13
And Joab drew nigh, and the people that were with him, unto the battle against the Syrians: and they fled before him.

2 Samuel 18:8
For the battle was there scattered over the face of all the country: and the wood devoured more people that day than the sword devoured.

2 Samuel 22:40
For thou hast girded me with strength to battle: them that rose up against me hast thou subdued under me.

1 Chronicles 19:14
So Joab and the people that were with him drew nigh before the Syrians unto the battle; and they fled before him.

2 Chronicles 14:10
Then Asa went out against him, and they set the battle in array in the valley of Zephathah at Mareshah.

Job 41:8
Lay thine hand upon him, remember the battle, do no more.

COMFORT | ˈkəmftərbəl |
providing physical ease and relaxation
: invitingly comfortable beds.

    We all search for COMFORT. COMFORTABLE clothes, COMFORTABLE shoes, COMFORTABLE chairs, COMFORTABLE relationships.
Being COMFORTABLE is one of our biggest necessities. With COMFORTABLE clothes we are able to move freely and take away the anxiety of eating that biscuit.
 With COMFORTABLE shoes we can walk a further distance or dance an extra song. In a COMFORTABLE relationship we can freely speak our mind without worrying if our mate will see us in an awkward way. When you're COMFORTABLE you tend to remove the restraint of your abilities.
What are some of the things you desire to make life more COMFORTABLE for you? Have you worked on the areas of life that can cause COMFORT of the soul?
A more COMFORTABLE home? What are some of the efforts you have made to create a COMFORTABLE state of mind? It's usually when DISCOMFORTS come along we tend to appreciate the COMFORT of what we have.

Isaiah 40:
Comfort ye, comfort ye my people, saith your God.

Matthew 5:4
Blessed are they that mourn: for they shall be comforted.

Isaiah 66:13
*As one whom his mother comforteth,
so will I comfort you;
and ye shall be comforted in Jerusalem.*

Jeremiah 8:18
When I would comfort myself against sorrow, my heart is faint in me.

1 Thessalonians 4:18
Wherefore comfort one another with these words.

2 Corinthians 1:4
who comforteth us in all our tribulation, that we may be able to comfort them which are in any trouble, by the comfort wherewith we ourselves are comforted of God.

Job 16:2
*I have heard many such things:
miserable comforters are ye all.*

Job 21:34
*How then comfort ye me in vain,
seeing in your answers there remaineth falsehood?*

Psalm 71:21
*Thou shalt increase my greatness,
and comfort me on every side.*

Psalm 94:19
*In the multitude of my thoughts within me
thy comforts delight my soul.*

Psalm 119:50
*This is my comfort in my affliction:
for thy word hath quickened me.*

Song of Solomon 2:5
*Stay me with flagons, comfort me with apples:
for I am sick of love.*

Acts 20:12
*And they brought the young man alive, and were not a little
comforted.*

Romans 1:12
*that is, that I may be comforted together with you by the mutual
faith both of you and me.*

1 Corinthians 14:3
*But he that prophesieth speaketh unto men to edification, and
exhortation, and comfort.*

1 Thessalonians 3:7
*therefore, brethren, we were comforted over you in all our affliction
and distress by your faith:*

2 Thessalonians 2:17
comfort your hearts, and stablish you in every good word and work.

Ecclesiastes 4:1
So I returned, and considered all the oppressions that are done under the sun: and behold the tears of such as were oppressed, and they had no comforter; and on the side of their oppressors there was power; but they had no comforter.

2 Corinthians 7:13
Therefore we were comforted in your comfort: yea, and exceedingly the more joyed we for the joy of Titus, because his spirit was refreshed by you all.

1 Corinthians 7:22
For he that is called in the Lord, being a servant, is the Lord's freeman: likewise also he that is called, being free, is Christ's servant.

Job 7:13
When I say, My bed shall comfort me, my couch shall ease my complaint;

Job 9:27
If I say, I will forget my complaint, I will leave off my heaviness, and comfort myself:

COMPASSION |kəmˈpa sh ən|
noun
sympathetic pity and concern for the sufferings or misfortunes of others :
the victims should be treated with compassion.

The Lord loves us with COMPASSION. It is His grace and mercy that wakes us in the morning and starts us on our way. The same COMPASSION of loving each other should be exemplified daily. Using a softer tone of our tongues as it reflects the TRUE feelings stored in our hearts. It takes an extra ordinary type of individual to go out of their way to help someone in need. It takes a COMPASSIONATE person to leave their comfort zone to assist when the tough times roll through like a surge in someone else's life.

I have been blessed to come across the paths of individuals that has made a conscious effort of giving back to those that need an extra hand when they seem to be down on their luck or experiencing a difficult spell that may be a test of their faith.

My grandfather, the late Rev. Jesse Lafayette, Sr. made it his life mission to assist anyone that he could along this journey we call life. He etched the phrase "It could be them today and you tomorrow" in my mind. Letting me know that no one ever volunteers to fall upon hardships. And maybe it could be the COMPASSION of a loved one, friend or even a complete stranger that could turn their situation around for the better. I encourage you today to think along the same lines. Challenge yourself to become more of a COMPASSIONATE person and help anyone that you can. Remember: "It could be them today and you tomorrow".

Jude 1:22
And of some have compassion, making a difference:

Psalm 118:11
They compassed me about; yea, they compassed me about: but in the name of the Lord I will destroy them.

Romans 9:15
For he saith to Moses, I will have mercy on whom I will have mercy, and I will have compassion on whom I will have compassion.

1 Samuel 23:21
And Saul said, Blessed be ye of the Lord; for ye have compassion on me.

Psalm 17:9
from the wicked that oppress me, from my deadly enemies, who compass me about.

Psalm 88:17
They came round about me daily like water; they compassed me about together.

Psalm 109:3
They compassed me about also with words of hatred; and fought against me without a cause.

Lamentations 3:5
He hath builded against me,
and compassed me with gall and travail.

Lamentations 3:22
It is of the Lord's mercies that we are not consumed,
because his compassions fail not.

Mark 8:2
I have compassion on the multitude, because they have now been
with me three days, and have nothing to eat:

1 Kings 7:24
And under the brim of it round about there were knops
compassing it, ten in a cubit, compassing the sea round about: the
knops were cast in two rows, when it was cast.

1 Kings 8:50
and forgive thy people that have sinned against thee, and all their
transgressions wherein they have transgressed against thee, and give
them compassion before them who carried them captive, that they may
have compassion on them:

2 Chronicles 4:3
And under it was the similitude of oxen, which did compass it
round about: ten in a cubit, compassing the sea round about. Two
rows of oxen were cast, when it was cast.

Joshua 6:11
So the ark of the Lord compassed the city, going about it once: and
they came into the camp, and lodged in the camp.

Joshua 6:14
And the second day they compassed the city once, and returned into the camp: so they did six days.

2 Samuel 22:5
When the waves of death compassed me, the floods of ungodly men made me afraid;

2 Samuel 22:6
the sorrows of hell compassed me about; the snares of death prevented me;

CONFESSION |kənˈfe sh ən|

a formal statement admitting that one is guilty of a crime

" Confession is good for the soul ."
Although it may not be easy to admit guilt on our end, speaking the hard details of truth that may display us in a different light can be quite difficult. It is easier to conceal our inner thoughts of truth and blend with the consensus to maintain a certain comfort level and avoid turmoil. When you think of CONFESSING your mind tends to gravitate towards revealing shameful or harmful information; Telling something to someone that may be hurt or affected by the facts you chose to conceal.
When you hear the phrase "CONFESSION is good for the soul" what comes to mind? What makes the soul so at ease or free by telling all? Is it better to come clean and let others be in the know to base their decisions on all of the facts at hand? Do you ever feel that applied pressure is the only way you will CONFESS?

John 1:20
And he confessed, and denied not; but confessed, I am not the Christ.

Matthew 3:6
and were baptized of him in Jordan, confessing their sins.

Matthew 10:32
Whosoever therefore shall confess me before men, him will I confess also before my Father which is in heaven.

Acts 19:18
And many that believed came, and confessed, and shewed their deeds.

Luke 12:18
And he said, This will I do: I will pull down my barns, and build greater; and there will I bestow all my fruits and my goods.

Nehemiah 9:2
And the seed of Israel separated themselves from all strangers, and stood and confessed their sins, and the iniquities of their fathers.

Mark 1:5
And there went out unto him all the land of Judæa, and they of Jerusalem, and were all baptized of him in the river of Jordan, confessing their sins.

Acts 23:8
For the Sadducees say that there is no resurrection, neither angel, nor spirit: but the Pharisees confess both.

Romans 10:10
For with the heart man believeth unto righteousness; and with the mouth confession is made unto salvation.

Philippians 2:11
and that every tongue should confess that Jesus Christ is Lord, to the glory of God the Father.

1 John 1:9
If we confess our sins, he is faithful and just to forgive us our sins, and to cleanse us from all unrighteousness.

Leviticus 5:5
And it shall be, when he shall be guilty in one of these things, that he shall confess that he hath sinned in that thing:

Leviticus 26:40
If they shall confess their iniquity, and the iniquity of their fathers, with their trespass which they trespassed against me, and that also they have walked contrary unto me;

Ezra 10:11
Now therefore make confession unto the Lord God of your fathers, and do his pleasure: and separate yourselves from the people of the land, and from the strange wives.

Job 40:14
Then will I also confess unto thee that thine own right hand can save thee.

Daniel 9:20
And whiles I was speaking, and praying, and confessing my sin and the sin of my people Israel, and presenting my supplication before the Lord my God for the holy mountain of my God;

John 9:22
These words spake his parents, because they feared the Jews: for the Jews had agreed already, that if any man did confess that he was Christ, he should be put out of the synagogue.

John 12:42
Nevertheless among the chief rulers also many believed on him; but because of the Pharisees they did not confess him, lest they should be put out of the synagogue:

Acts 24:14
But this I confess unto thee, that after the way which they call heresy, so worship I the God of my fathers, believing all things which are written in the law and in the prophets:

Romans 14:11
For it is written, As I live, saith the Lord, every knee shall bow to me, and every tongue shall confess to God.

CONFLICT | ˈkänˌflikt |
a serious disagreement or argument, typically a protracted one :
a prolonged armed struggle

Initially CONFLICT may not be thought of in a positive light. Being that two or more odds are at hand procrastinating a unified decision or result of agreement. What are some of the CONFLICTS you have dealt with recently? Be it at work, home, church or even in the simple task of planning a day out with a friend for lunch. CONFLICT of opinions, CONFLICTS of schedules. CONFLICTS = differences. With a little patience, understanding and reasoning along with strategic planning CONFLICT can easily lead to resolution.

The law of the land as we know it now has been shaped in some form or fashion due to the result of a CONFLICT. Recognize that differences of opinions and the adaption of the solution that best fit for that situation can defuse the problem. It is important to build CONFLICT resolution skills to cope and reason in a positive way and not let CONFLICTS of opinions lead to an insensible result that is the blame for so many senseless deaths and grudges held within the community today.

Psa 55:9
Confuse them, O Lord! Frustrate their plans! 2 For I see violence and conflict in the city.

Psa 140:2
who plan ways to harm me. All day long they stir up conflict.

Hab 1:3
Why do you force me to witness injustice? Why do you put up with wrongdoing? Destruction and violence confront me; conflict is present and one must endure strife.

Phi 1:30
since you are encountering the same conflict that you saw me face and now hear that I am facing.

Heb 10:32
But remember the former days when you endured a harsh conflict of suffering after you were enlightened.

CONSISTENCY |kənˈsistənsē|

the trend shows a degree of consistency uniformity, constancy, regularity, evenness, steadiness, stability, equilibrium; dependability, reliability.

Often we set goals and attempt to achieve them in sporadic spells. Almost as if things will come into place with little to no effort or maybe even a lucky end of the bargain. If life were that simple every testimony would be a success story. No struggle, no stop and start overs, no competition and no reason to aim higher. With every success story you will find a pattern or a routine that was diligently sought with sheer CONSISTENCY. To be the best at whatever it is you would like to accomplish in life you must set goals, map out a plan and follow it to the road of completion.

Be so CONSISTENT along your journey that your words and intentions are never far off the mark and coincide with the vision God has placed in your heart.

You can CONSTANTLY complain that things aren't going well; life isn't what you expected it to be; and add another million things to your gripe party, or CONSISTENTLY work towards becoming a better person by aiming higher, holding yourself to standards and meeting deadlines day in and day out while attempting to CONSTANTLY march to higher grounds.

DECISION [dih-sizh-uhn]

the act or process of deciding; determination, as of a question or doubt, by making a judgment:

> They must make a decision between these two contestants.

Life is filled with DECISIONS. Now or later? Yes or no? Leave or stay? The list grows with the more growth we encounter throughout our lives.

The DECISIONS we make can be wavered by many variables. Wanting instant gratification or enduring the circumstance for an elongated milestone. Our CHARACTER is often attached to the DECISIONS we make as we often hear the reference of others opinions of us primarily based on the DECISIONS we have made or even the DECISIONS we did not make. With so many obstacles we face daily it is important to wake up and DECIDE to have a great day. Distractions and disappointments will exist and show up like clockwork, but how you DECIDE to react to them will ultimately determine the outcome to the situation.

DECIDE to be the best version of yourself that you can be. DECIDE to make the sacrifices that will strengthen you spiritually, mentally and physically. DECIDE to be a better friend, a better family, a better influence on those you interact with. DECIDE to make the best of every challenge that comes your way.

1 Kings 20:40

And as thy servant was busy here and there, he was gone. And the king of Israel said unto him, So shall thy judgment be; thyself hast decided it.

Joel 3:14

Multitudes, multitudes in the valley of decision: for the day of the Lord is near in the valley of decision.

DEFINITION | ˌdefəˈni sh ən |
an exact statement or description of the nature, scope, or meaning of something :
the degree of distinctness in outline of an object, image, or sound ;

What is your DEFINITION?
What characteristics distinguish you from the next individual? What DEFINES you? In ten words are less how would you sum up the mold of the person you are. Far too often we attempt to find the recipe that makes others what and who they are, never spending time to label our own ingredients. The DECISIONS we make are a reflection of our subconscious. The friends we keep, our reactions during adversities and our sources of motivation all DEFINES us. We all should strive for those DEFINING moments of life. The pivotal moment when our DECISIONS and opportunity meet and the road takes a drastic turn.
The time will come when our DEFINITION will speak for us before our words will be able to. Are you sending the proper interpretation of who and what you truly are? Today's assignment: Take a few moments and think of a few words that DEFINE you. Determine which are worth keeping and which you are willing to part ways with in an effort to become a better you.

DEPRESSION | ˌdespəˈrā sh ən |
a state of despair, typically one that results in rash or extreme behavior :

DESPERATION is the ground we stand in our time of despair. Seemingly leaving us with the option of hopelessness or rash action of surviving by any means necessary. While dark clouds may arise and visions begin to fade and reality presents a harsh blow, panic is only a natural reaction. DESPERATION will make the most sound of mind being believe that the unthinkable of actions may be the only way to survive or keep your head above drowning waters even if it's for a day longer. Being in a comfortable position today we can say "what we would not stoop to doing". In the state of DESPERATION we are put to the test of dealing with circumstance and our ability to flex patience and depend on God's grace to move us to a higher level from which we are feeling the wrath of the valley's lows. Give a little thought of the most uncontrollable predicaments that would place you in a state of DESPERATION. Are you prayed up enough to stand still and be DESPERATE only for God's help? Or would you become DESPERATE enough to lean towards your own understandings of momentary reasons.

Gen 30:8
Then Rachel said, "I have fought a desperate struggle with my sister, but I have won." So she named him Naphtali.

Exo 2:23
During that long period of time the king of Egypt died, and the Israelites groaned because of the slave labor. They cried out, and their desperate cry because of their slave labor went up to God.

1Ki 8:28
But respond favorably to your servant's prayer and his request for help, O Lord my God. Answer the desperate prayer your servant is presenting to you today.

2Ch 6:19
But respond favorably to your servant's prayer and his request for help, O Lord my God. Answer the desperate prayer your servant is presenting to you.

DETERMINATION |di͵tərməˈnā sh ən|

firmness of purpose; resoluteness
: he advanced with an unflinching determination.

"Goals in life all begin with a vision. Goals in life are met by DETERMINATION." Behind all success is a path that can be traced with faith disappointments, and even a few uncertainties. You are placed in a position that has been designed specifically for you. No guarantees that it will be understood or clear from the beginning, but the more you trod the pavement and are faced with opportunities you begin to understand by and by the steps that needs to be taken.
Now you find yourself standing seemingly miles from the destination you know you are able to be with persistence and determination. Great accomplishments before, during and even after our time will always be tracked and traced by pavement that has been paved. The race is ran at different paces and perhaps even different directions but they are only completed with the forward motion.

Deu 17:10
You must then do as they have determined at that place the Lord chooses. Be careful to do just as you are taught.

Jos 11:20
for the Lord determined to make them obstinate so they would attack Israel. He wanted Israel to annihilate them without mercy, as he had instructed Moses.

Jdg 9:8
"The trees were determined to go out and choose a king for themselves. They said to the olive tree, 'Be our king!'

Rut 1:18
When Naomi realized that Ruth was determined to go with her, she stopped trying to dissuade her.

1Ki 20:40
Well, it just so happened that while your servant was doing this and that, he disappeared." The king of Israel said to him, "Your punishment is already determined by your own testimony."

1Ki 20:42
The prophet then said to him, "This is what the Lord says, 'Because you released a man I had determined should die, you will pay with your life and your people will suffer instead of his people."

2Ki 11:1
When Athaliah the mother of Ahaziah saw that her son was dead, she was determined to destroy the entire royal line.

2Ch 3:3
Solomon laid the foundation for God's temple; its length (determined according to the old standard of measure) was 90 feet, and its width 30 feet.

2Ch 11:16
Those among all the Israelite tribes who were determined to worship the Lord God of Israel followed them to Jerusalem to sacrifice to the Lord God of their ancestors.

2Ch 12:14
He did evil because he was not determined to follow the Lord.

DEFINITION | ˌdefəˈni sh ən |
an exact statement or description of the nature, scope, or meaning of something :
the degree of distinctness in outline of an object, image, or sound ;

What is your DEFINITION?
What characteristics distinguish you from the next individual? What defines you? In ten words are less how would you sum up the mold of the person you are. Far too often we attempt to find the recipe that makes others what and who they are, never spending time to label our own ingredients. The decisions we make are a reflection of our subconscious. The friends we keep, our reactions during adversities and our sources of motivation all defines us. We all should strive for those defining moments of life. The pivotal moment when our decisions and opportunity meet and the road takes a drastic turn. The time will come when our definition will speak for us before our words will be able to. Are you sending the proper interpretation of who and what you truly are? Today's assignment: Take a few moments and think of a few words that DEFINE you. determine which are worth keeping and which you are willing to part ways with in an effort to become a better you.

DEPRESSION | di'pre sh ən

severe despondency and dejection, typically felt over a period of time and accompanied by feelings of hopelessness and inadequacy.

    DEPRESSION is something that causes an effect on not only the person going through an issue but others that care for you and want to help you through the struggles. One thing that must not go under the radar is that DEPRESSION does not discriminate. Any age, ethnicity back ground or financial standings can be affected. Studies show that teenage suicide rates have risen in astonishing rates over the past decade. Have things really changed so drastically over the years to where we feel as if we cannot cope with the challenges of life?
Or have our mentalities changed to where our challenges and changes of life have let our DEPRESSION take our minds and souls to a level that we dare not cope with the issues at hand but result to a permanent solution for a temporary problem. DEPRESSION should not be viewed as a sign of weakness. One should not be ashamed to seek spiritual guidance to fight the strong hold and even counseling from someone who is open minded to helping you see things clearly.
Listing reasons you feel are legitimately worthy of being DEPRESSED behind is a shorter list than the reasons you have not to be DEPRESSED.

1 Samuel 16:14

Now the Spirit of the Lord had left Saul, and the Lord sent a tormenting spirit that filled him with depression and fear.

Job 30:16

"And now my life seeps away. Depression haunts my days."

Psalm 143:7

Come quickly, Lord, and answer me, for my depression deepens. Don't turn away from me, or I will die.

DESPERATION | ˌdespəˈrāshən |
a state of despair, typically one that results in rash or extreme behavior :

DESPERATION is the ground we stand in our time of DESPAIR. Seemingly leaving us with the option of hopelessness or rash action of surviving by any means necessary. While dark clouds may arise and visions begin to fade and reality presents a harsh blow, panic is only a natural reaction. DESPERATION will make the most sound of mind being believe that the unthinkable of actions may be the only way to survive or keep your head above drowning waters even if it's for a day longer. Being in a comfortable position today we can say "what we would not stoop to doing". In the state of DESPERATION we are put to the test of dealing with circumstance and our ability to flex patience and depend on God's grace to move us to a higher level from which we are feeling the wrath of the valley's lows. Give a little thought of the most uncontrollable predicaments that would place you in a state of DESPERATION. Are you prayed up enough to stand still and be DESPERATE only for God's help? Or would you become DESPERATE enough to lean towards your own understandings of momentary reasons.

Gen 30:8
Then Rachel said, "I have fought a desperate struggle with my sister, but I have won." 1 So she named him Naphtali. 2

Exo 2:23
1 During 2 that long period of time 3 the king of Egypt died, and the Israelites 4 groaned because of the slave labor. They cried out, and their desperate cry 5 because of their slave labor went up to God.

1Ki 8:28
But respond favorably to 1 your servant's prayer and his request for help, O Lord my God. Answer 2 the desperate prayer 3 your servant is presenting to you 4 today.

2Ch 6:19
But respond favorably to 1 your servant's prayer and his request for help, O Lord my God. Answer 2 the desperate prayer 3 your servant is presenting to you. 4

Jer 19:9
I will reduce the people of this city to desperate straits during the siege imposed on it by their enemies who are seeking to kill them. I will make them so desperate that they will eat the flesh of their own sons and daughters and

DETERMINATION |di͵tərməˈnā sh ən|
firmness of purpose; resoluteness :
he advanced with an unflinching determination.

"Goals in life all begin with a vision. Goals in life are met by DETERMINATION." Behind all success is a path that can be traced with faith, disappointments and even a few uncertainties. You are placed in a position that has been designed specifically for you. No guarantees that it will be understood or clear from the beginning, but the more you trod the pavement and are faced with opportunities you begin to understand by and by the steps that needs to be taken.

Now you find yourself standing seemingly miles from the destination you know you are ABLE to be with persistence and DETERMINATION. Great accomplishments before, during and even after our time will always be tracked and traced by pavement that has been paved. The race is ran at different paces and perhaps even different directions but they are only completed with the forward motion.

Deu 17:10
You must then do as they have determined at that place the Lord chooses. Be careful to do just as you are taught.

Jos 11:20
for the Lord determined to make them obstinate so they would attack Israel. He wanted Israel to annihilate them without mercy, as he had instructed Moses.

Jdg 9:8
"The trees were determined to go out and choose a king for themselves. They said to the olive tree, 'Be our king!'

Rut 1:18
When Naomi realized that Ruth was determined to go with her, she stopped trying to dissuade her.

1Ki 20:40
Well, it just so happened that while your servant was doing this and that, he disappeared." The king of Israel said to him, "Your punishment is already determined by your own testimony."

1Ki 20:42
The prophet then said to him, "This is what the Lord says, 'Because you released a man I had determined should die, you will pay with your life and your people will suffer instead of his people.'"

2Ki 11:1
When Athaliah the mother of Ahaziah saw that her son was dead, she was determined to destroy the entire royal line.

2Ch 3:3
Solomon laid the foundation for God's temple; its length (determined according to the old standard of measure) was 90 feet, and its width 30 feet.

2Ch 11:16
Those among all the Israelite tribes who were determined to worship the Lord God of Israel followed them to Jerusalem to sacrifice to the Lord God of their ancestors.

2Ch 12:14
He did evil because he was not determined to follow the Lord.

DISCIPLINE | ˈdisəplin |
the practice of training people to obey rules or a code of behavior, using punishment to correct disobedience

DISCIPLINE. A word that carries the weight of champions. For one to be DISCIPLINED they must make sacrifices. To give of your desires and focus on what will make you better than you were yesterday and greater than you will be tomorrow. DISCIPLINE is an example of self-control, a sense of obedience.

With every action there is a reaction. DISCIPLINE should be used accordingly to balance a happy medium of sorts. Where there is no structure things tend not to get completed or fall out of line.

When a child displays improper behavior a parent will correct them with DISCIPLINARY actions. The same mind set of correcting our improper behavior should fall in place as we fall off track.

Courses change and the current of life can sway us from the path we intended to take. We should practice DISCIPLINE within our daily routines and hold ourselves accountable for the choices we make and the amount of sacrifices we put in gearing towards the rewards we expect in return.

Job 36:10
He openeth also their ear to discipline, and commandeth that they return from iniquity.

ENCOURAGE |en'kərij
give support, confidence, or hope to (someone)

To ENCOURAGE is to inspire. Life or death lies within the power of the tongue. How do you utilize your power? Is it used to uplift your family and friends? Or do you take that time to remind them of the negative breakdowns that may be presenting challenges?
An ENCOURAGING word may be the inspiration someone needs to get through a trying day. The devil comes to steal your joy and to discourage you right when you are ready to break through the bondage that has held you captive for so long. ENCOURAGEMENT keeps you motivated when your turn to get off the bench and enter the game does not seem to come fast enough. ENCOURAGEMENT gives you the inspiration to wait a little longer and practice a little harder in anticipation for the time the coach calls on you to hit the court and make the difference. ENCOURAGING someone to keep their chin up and hold their head up high when they feel as if things are not going their way is an example of love.
 There is no need to remind you of all the things that went wrong in the final seconds before the buzzard sounds and the crowd leaves. But to ENCOURAGE you and make you want to go back and give the crowd a reason to cheer is a gift of hope that will push you a little harder to be that much better.

Today, I ENCOURAGE you to ENCOURAGE someone else.

2 Chronicles 35:2

And he set the priests in their charges, and encouraged them to the service of the house of the Lord,

Deuteronomy 1:38

But Joshua the son of Nun, which standeth before thee, he shall go in thither: encourage him: for he shall cause Israel to inherit it.

Deuteronomy 3:28

But charge Joshua, and encourage him, and strengthen him: for he shall go over before this people, and he shall cause them to inherit the land which thou shalt see.

Judges 20:22

And the people the men of Israel encouraged themselves, and set their battle again in array in the place where they put themselves in array the first day.

2 Chronicles 31:4

Moreover he commanded the people that dwelt in Jerusalem to give the portion of the priests and the Levites, that they might be encouraged in the law of the Lord.

Psalms 64:5

They encourage themselves in an evil matter: they commune of laying snares privily; they say, Who shall see them?

Isaiah 41:7

So the carpenter encouraged the goldsmith, and he that smootheth with the hammer him that smote the anvil, saying, It is ready for the sodering: and he fastened it with nails, that it should not be moved.

1 Samuel 30:6

And David was greatly distressed; for the people spake of stoning him, because the soul of all the people was grieved, every man for his sons and for his daughters: but David encouraged himself in the Lord his God.

2 Samuel 11:25

Then David said unto the messenger, Thus shalt thou say unto Joab, Let not this thing displease thee, for the sword devoureth one as well as another: make thy battle more strong against the city, and overthrow it: and encourage thou him.

ENERGY [en-er-jee]

The capacity for vigorous activity; available power: I eat chocolate to get quick energy.

the strength and vitality required for sustained physical or mental activity

There are only twenty-four hours in each of the seven days of the week. No matter how you attempt to squeeze things in or balance things out to measure time, it is a must that you make time to rest and replenish your ENERGY.
You can't be of much assistance to anyone else if you don't take the time to care for yourself. Why do we waste so much time and ENERGY focusing on the little things that at the end of the day will not enhance our lives? Such as the water cooler talk, simple minded gossip, idle hands that are ultimately the devil's work shop. Instead, let's make a conscious effort to use our ENERGY to be a positive force to those around us. Let your ENERGY attract like ENERGY and all the goodness thereof. Day by day you will discover that negative forces begin to vanish as there is no room there for the dreary vibes it brings. Revitalize your mind, body and soul. Build your ENERGY with a motivational moment. Let your ENERGY determine the outcome of your day.

EVALUATION |iˈvalyoō ˌāt|
form an idea of the amount, number, or value of;

How honest are you willing to be with yourself right now? If I were to ask you to hold a self-EVALUATION how many corners would you cut to disguise the truth? To EVALUATE is to form an idea of the amount, number or value of;
Are you willing to come to grasp with the true you?
Step back and view yourself through the eyes of others. What is it that they see when they look at you? What body language are you giving when someone asks for your help? Is it a quick response of a willingness to help? Or is it a cold shoulder of resentment for even asking?
What is it that they hear when they ask for your advice? Is it a loving tone of concernment? Or is it a spiteful tongue of "Well, that's what you get!"
Evaluate where you are in life verses where you want to be in life. What are you doing to accomplish your goals and reach the next level? Evaluate your daily decisions and see if your goals are stagnated because your efforts are not adding up. Evaluate the company you keep. I was told that people do one of two things; they either add or subtract to your well-being. It is up to us to make decisions on the company that we keep. Evaluate the motives of those in your circle. Everyone in your presence my not necessarily be in your corner cheering with your best interest at heart. Evaluate every outcome of the decisions you make and honestly say if you are willing to deal with consequences to follow. Make today a day of evaluation. Use whatever grading system works best for you. Tackle the angles of life that matters the most to you and encourage a friend to do a self-EVALUATION today as well.

EVOLVE |iˈvälv|

> develop gradually, esp. from a simple to a more complex form

EVOLUTION is a change that happens whether we are ready for it or not. The makings of who and what we become is a part of the molding process that shapes us into the person that we are. It's a part of life that I believe we may contribute a bigger role than we take credit for. "Surround yourself with yourself" a phrase that sounds quite vague but yet has some depth to it. EVOLUTION is not a change that takes place over night, but is a transformation that occurs from a simplistic state to a complex form that has been nurtured and molded. As we EVOLVE from a physical standpoint let us also focus on the EVOLUTION of our mental and spiritual capacity. What your mentality embraces is what it will shape and exemplify. What your spirituality is fed will be displayed during the trials that will take place during your EVOLUTION. Take a moment to reflect over your life. As you have EVOLVED over the years what changes have been made? Do you see a pattern in the people, habits or places that has remained the same or have altered throughout the years? Where do you see yourself in the next five years? From now to then, what are some things that will be a staple or will hinder your EVOLUTION? Are you ready to make the necessary adjustments? How ready are you to EVOLVE?

FAITH | faɪθ |
strong belief in God
complete trust or confidence in someone or something

    FAITH is like the wind. Although we cannot touch, taste or even see the wind we somehow believe that it is there. It's the string of hope that encourages you to keep pushing towards the mark you have envisioned yourself reaching. With all of the tangibles that linger throughout your journey, faith is the whisper of encouragement giving you a slight direction. At the point you feel as if you are against all odds and there is nothing left but a smidge of hope it's FAITH that reassure that your works are not in vain.
Often we find ourselves placing our FAITH into people and items. Once they let us down it serves as a reminder to place it where it should have been in the first place.
With FAITH the size of a mustard seed we shall be able to move mountains and conquer the world. Some days it is only FAITH that there is something greater than what meet the eyes that keeps you going when you seem to be on your last leg of the race. FAITH is just like a muscle. The more you use it the stronger it becomes. If everything went our way on our time all of the time there wouldn't be much need for FAITH. Adversities come not to hinder us but to bring us closer to the source that strengthens us.
With FAITH in God, all things are possible.

Vision(FAITH +ENDURANCE)= PROSPERITY

Galatians 3:9
So then they which be of faith are blessed with faithful Abraham.

2 Corinthians 1:24
Not for that we have dominion over your faith, but are helpers of your joy: for by faith ye stand.

Hebrews 3:2
Who was faithful to him that appointed him, as also Moses was faithful in all his house.

Galatians 3:25
But after that faith is come, we are no longer under a schoolmaster.

1 Timothy 4:9
This is a faithful saying and worthy of all acceptation.

1 Timothy 5:12
Having damnation, because they have cast off their first faith.

Luke 16:10
He that is faithful in that which is least is faithful also in much: and he that is unjust in the least is unjust also in much.

Romans 3:30
Seeing it is one God, which shall justify the circumcision by faith, and uncircumcision through faith.

FOREVER | fəˈrevər; fô- |
for all future time; for always

    When we say FOREVER do we take into account that it means for a very long time? God's love for you and I is FOREVER. There is no beginning nor is there an ending to the limit of time that we are allowed the grace and love of our merciful heavenly Father.
There are no conditions or boundaries that will alter how long He will take us under His wing. His words and promises will FOREVER remain the same.
Power lies within the words we speak. As we release our words into the atmosphere we should hold accountability of the force behind the message we are sending.
When we make promises of FOREVER are we willing to take the challenges, tasks and obstacles that we will encounter along the way? To endure hardships on earth and focus our ambitions of striving to please God to spend eternity in the heavens which have been prepared for us, we should focus on spreading goodness FOREVER.
With the promise of FOREVER there will be more obstacles to face and hurdles to jump. The longer you remain on that path is the more ground you will cover. When you opt the FOREVER mode in an area of life, remember the short cut is not what you are signing up for.

FORGIVE |fər'giv|

to cease to feel resentment against: to forgive one's enemies.

*For giving may be the gift needed the most. *

Forgiving someone who may have hurt you intentionally or unknowingly is a hurdle that can take effort. Before we are ABLE to stop feeling angry or resentful towards someone for an offense, flaw, or mistake, we have to put our hurt to the side and recognize that the love of the Lord will mend what was torn.

Forgiveness is deeper than saying "I forgive you." It is the ability to release the resentment of the hurt that was inflicted upon you and to carry on with love and compassion for the inflictor.

In order for us to FORGIVE someone we must first experience some sort of hurt, neglect or even betrayal. It takes every ounce of being to evaporate and being consumed by a higher force to release the feeling of hurt and shame giving you strength to move on as everything is back to normal or to a point of normalcy to function in harmony. It's only human nature to feel resentment towards someone who has demonstrated ill will towards you. FORGIVENESS is possibly the most ultimate test of being a child of God. As He FORGAVE all whom have fallen short be it intentional or not.

John 8:7
So when they continued asking him, he lifted up himself, and said unto them, He that is without sin among you, let him first cast a stone at her.

No one on this earth is perfect and we all have made mistakes. As we will need FORGIVENESS from those we have wronged let us not forget to exemplify the same characteristics of FORGIVENESS towards the next.

It may not be easy but it is definitely a must as we are made in His image and likeness thereof.

Matthew 6:14-15
For if you forgive men when they sin against you, your heavenly Father will also forgive you. But if you do not forgive men their sins, your Father will not forgive your sins.

1 John 1:9
If we confess our sins, he is faithful and just and will forgive us our sins and purify us from all unrighteousness.

Isaiah 43:25-26
"I, even I, am he who blots out your transgressions, for my own sake, and remembers your sins no more. Review the past for me, let us argue the matter together; state the case for your innocence.

Acts 3:19
Repent, then, and turn to God, so that your sins may be wiped out, that times of refreshing may come from the Lord,

Isaiah 1:18
"Come now, let us reason together," says the LORD. "Though your sins are like scarlet, they shall be as white as snow; though they are red as crimson, they shall be like wool.

2 Corinthians 5:17
Therefore, if anyone is in Christ, he is a new creation; the old has gone, the new has come!

Ephesians 1:7
In him we have redemption through his blood, the forgiveness of sins, in accordance with the riches of God's grace

Hebrews 10:17
Then he adds: "Their sins and lawless acts I will remember no more."

Daniel 9:9
The Lord our God is merciful and forgiving, even though we have rebelled against him;

Colossians 1:13-14
For he has rescued us from the dominion of darkness and brought us into the kingdom of the Son he loves, in whom we have redemption, the forgiveness of sins.

Psalm 103:12
as far as the east is from the west, so far has he removed our transgressions from us.

Numbers 14:19-21
In accordance with your great love, forgive the sin of these people, just as you have pardoned them from the time they left Egypt until now." The LORD replied, "I have forgiven them, as you asked. Nevertheless, as surely as I live and as surely as the glory of the LORD fills the whole earth,

GLORY | ˈglôrē |
high renown or honor won by notable achievements

To bask in our own GLORY is unpleasing in the sight of God. All that we are, in all that we do He is to be praised. Often we find ourselves getting wrapped up in the preconceived notion that it is all within our power to unlock the doors to our success. Although our decision making process plays a key factor, God has already laid the blue print to our destiny. For every trial give God the GLORY. For every miracle give God the GLORY. For everything that has breath has been placed on this earth to GLORIFY Him.

Your abilities, possessions and even your talents are yours due to the fact God has allowed them to be utilized by you to enhance your life. Trusting that your desire to please Him will lead you to make the right decision and set an example leading others to His kingdom so they may give all the honor, power, praise and GLORY as it was intended to be from the beginning of time.

1 Thessalonians 2:20
For ye are our glory and joy.

Psalms 24:10
Who is this King of glory? The Lord of hosts, he is the King of glory. Selah.

2 Corinthians 11:18
Seeing that many glory after the flesh, I will glory also.

1 Corinthians 1:29
That no flesh should glory in his presence.

1 Corinthians 15:41
There is one glory of the sun, and another glory of the moon, and another glory of the stars: for one star differeth from another star in glory.

2 Corinthians 10:17
But he that glorieth, let him glory in the Lord.

Galatians 1:5
To whom be glory for ever and ever. Amen.

Proverbs 25:27
It is not good to eat much honey: so for men to search their own glory is not glory.

John 7:18
He that speaketh of himself seeketh his own glory: but he that seeketh his glory that sent him, the same is true, and no unrighteousness is in him.

2 Corinthians 3:9
For if the ministration of condemnation be glory, much more doth the ministration of righteousness exceed in glory.
crown from my head.

GOALS |gōl|

the object of a person's ambition or effort; an aim or desired result : going to law school has become the most important goal in his life.

Setting a GOAL is placing a marker on your vision. GOALS are best defined as **G**oing **O**ver **A**ll **L**ittle **S**teps that will lead you in the direction of where you want to be. Our path on this journey of life will experience obstacles that will take us for a loop from time to time.
Without a GOAL it is nearly impossible to pick up the pieces and move forward, for the final destination has not been made clear. Without a GOAL we spend countless hours roaming in circles and occupying our time with going with the motion. As children we are taught to work hard and accomplish the GOALS that have been set in place for us. In order to fulfill small or large GOALS a valiant effort must be made. It is never too late to start setting GOALS. Ask yourself, "where would I like to see myself in the future?" Are your current actions leading you closer to that GOAL? What changes would you like to make in order to accommodate the efforts of reaching your GOAL? Are you willing to make the necessary changes and stick with the modifications? Challenge yourself to better yourself one day at a time and start by Going Over All Little Steps that will lead you closer to the finish line.

GOD [god]

the one Supreme Being, the creator and ruler of the universe.

When asked "Who is GOD?" what is your immediate response? Set aside the labeling of any particular religion and ponder solely on the question "Who or what is GOD?"

Is the GOD you identify the God you exemplify? Your way of talking, your actions your daily routine... Is it all aligned with the GOD who is that of LOVE?

GOD the creator of all things wonderfully made in His image.

GOD the artist who designed the stars to shine brightly in the sky.

GOD the giver of life abundantly.

GOD the great I AM.

GOD the King of kings.

GOD the beginning and the ending.

It is easy to identify that which has been taught to us as GOD. Is it as easy to see the resemblance of GOD in your image?

GOD desires to be praised by you and longs to have a one on one relationship with you. He is the only one that can provide your every need.

Do you find yourself praising your job, earthly possessions and other obligations as your god? Before we get pulled into a direction of serving distractions let us build a stronger connection with God.

HAPPINESS | ˈhapē |
feeling or showing pleasure or contentment

Happiness can be found from the simple JOYS of life. The smiles we render to the unsuspecting to brighten their day or the random act of KINDNESS that warrants no bearing of debt of any sort of way. Too often we confuse HAPPINESS with the circumstances that come and go with an encounter of brief relief. Allowing our HAPPINESS to be DETERMINED by the situation at hand. Leaving your HAPPINESS in the hands of others can often leave you disappointed as they may be unaware of your dependency of their role in your expectancies. Let's not be so quick to thrive for a source that may not be sure of how to make themselves HAPPY. The ultimate source of where all JOY and HAPPINESS comes is beyond the skies. Anchor yourself in the Lord and may you experience the truth of the HAPPINNESS you have deserved from the beginning of time.

HEALING [hee-ling]

curing or curative; prescribed or helping to heal.

HEALING the process of mending. The bondage of damages that have occurred due to seen or unforeseen activities.

Before we are able to resend to the point of HEALING we must visit a destination that has placed us in some form of discomfort. A broken heart, a bruised shin, a shattered emotional state of mind. Different levels of pain calls for different levels of HEALING. With physical issues the diagnosis of HEALING time may be estimated by case studies of issues with similarities. Dealing with emotional pain and scars HEALING becomes more difficult to predict when it calls for recovery time. Once we have been emotionally tied to a connection and it is broken, a lack of trust or security are factors that must be identified and addressed before we can properly begin to HEAL. Acknowledging the issue and accepting the pain allows us to put our best foot forward on the road as we head to a HEALING with our name on it.

Exodus 15:26
He said, "If you listen carefully to the voice of the LORD your God and do what is right in his eyes, if you pay attention to his commands and keep all his decrees, I will not bring on you any of the diseases I brought on the Egyptians, for I am the LORD, who heals you."

Psalm 30:2
O LORD my God, I called to you for help and you healed me.

Isaiah 53:4-5
Surely he took up our infirmities and carried our sorrows, yet we considered him stricken by God, smitten by him, and afflicted. But he was pierced for our transgressions, he was crushed for our iniquities; the punishment that brought us peace was upon him, and by his wounds we are healed.

Psalm 147:3
He heals the brokenhearted and binds up their wounds.

Jeremiah 17:14
Heal me, O LORD, and I will be healed; save me and I will be saved, for you are the one I praise.

Matthew 9:35
Jesus went through all the towns and villages, teaching in their synagogues, preaching the good news of the kingdom and healing every disease and sickness.

1 Peter 2:24
He himself bore our sins in his body on the tree, so that we might die to sins and live for righteousness; by his wounds you have been healed.

Proverbs 4:20-22
My son, pay attention to what I say; listen closely to my words. Do not let them out of your sight, keep them within your heart; for they are life to those who find them and health to a man's whole body.

HOPE |hōp|
a feeling of expectation and desire for a certain thing to happen :
he looked through her belongings in the hope of coming across some information
I had high hopes of making the Olympic team.

Hebrews 11:1
"Now FAITH is the substance of things HOPED for, the evidence of things not seen."

A scripture that speaks volumes on the importance of believing that the light at the end of the tunnel is brighter than the fog of doubt portrays. At times challenges will arise and the obstacles may seem to be a burden too much to handle alone. That is why it is such a relief in knowing that our heavenly Father has an open ear to our open heart. With every dream and HOPE there is a believer attached. With the HOPE of being great and doing great things, there is an amount of unmeasured effort that goes hand in hand to support the cause. HOPE without the effort won't get you further than the mere dream of what could ultimately be your reality. Let HOPE be a driving force in your daily thought process that will keep you motivated enough to move closer to the destination you have HOPED to travel.

Job 17:15
And where is now my hope? as for my hope, who shall see it?

Lamentations 3:21
This I recall to my mind, therefore have I hope.

Romans 5:4
And patience, experience; and experience, hope:

Romans 8:24
For we are saved by hope: but hope that is seen is not hope: for what a man seeth, why doth he yet hope for?

Job 6:20
They were confounded because they had hoped; they came thither, and were ashamed.

Lamentations 3:18
And I said, My strength and my hope is perished from the Lord:

Lamentations 3:29
He putteth his mouth in the dust; if so be there may be hope.

1 Corinthians 15:19
If in this life only we have hope in Christ, we are of all men most miserable.

Galatians 5:5
For we through the Spirit wait for the hope of righteousness by faith.

1 Corinthians 9:10
Or saith he it altogether for our sakes? For our sakes, no doubt, this is written: that he that ploweth should plow in hope; and that he that thresheth in hope should be partaker of his hope.

Job 5:16
So the poor hath hope, and iniquity stoppeth her mouth.

Job 6:11
What is my strength, that I should hope? and what is mine end, that I should prolong my life?

Job 7:6
My days are swifter than a weaver's shuttle, and are spent without hope.

Job 8:13
So are the paths of all that forget God; and the hypocrite's hope shall perish:

Psalms 31:24
Be of good courage, and he shall strengthen your heart, all ye that hope in the Lord.

Psalms 39:7
And now, Lord, what wait I for? my hope is in thee.

HOSTILITY |hä'stilitē|
hostile behavior; unfriendliness or opposition :

Generations today seemingly carry a level of HOSTILITY beyond belief. News headlines, crime statistics and daily encounters show more HOSTILE behavior than ever. Why is everyone so angry?
Why do they take their frustration out in such a violent rage? Why do we carry such HOSTILITY in our hearts? When someone presents us with a confrontational manor are we equipped mentally to handle it in a mature way? Where does this HOSTILITY stem from? Usually when someone disrespects us we form an attitude of resentment. Which in return becomes emotions that are not processed in a healthy way. The lack of communication is causing harm that is deeper than what meets the eye. When people are unable to suppress their anger things tend to escalate and end with a very detrimental outcome.
HOSTILITY is a burden much heavier than we should volunteer to carry. Do not anchor yourself in ill will and sink your teeth into the bitterness of HOSTILITY. Pray without ceasing and ask God to search your heart and remove the anger, hurt and resentment that has allowed you to turn a pebble into a boulder. Release the HOSTILITY and set yourself free and find yourself closer to the God you serve.

HUMBLE | ˈhəmbəl |

having or showing a modest or low estimate of one's own importance
of low social, administrative, or political rank : she came from a humble, unprivileged background.

A HUMBLE heart is of good character. In everything that we do it should be done with a modest tone. Actions carried out with a boastful tone can be viewed as insincere and even miss the mark of which we were aiming. In all things that we do all glory should be given to our heavenly Father as it is His will and by His grace that we are able to receive and bestow blessings. Never let arrogance malice your heart and place you on a pedestal where you are higher than the next individual or even a god in your own eyes. Humble yourself at all times unto Christ and remember He is in control at all times. Show your heart HUMBLE and encourage others to bless in HUMBLENESS.

Proverbs 3:34
The Lord mocks proud mockers but gives grace to the humble.

Exodus 10:3
And Moses and Aaron came in unto Pharaoh, and said unto him, Thus saith the LORD God of the Hebrews, How long wilt thou refuse to humble thyself before me? let my people go, that they may serve me.

Leviticus 26:41
And that I also have walked contrary unto them, and have brought them into the land of their enemies; if then their uncircumcised hearts be humbled, and they then accept of the punishment of their iniquity:

Deuteronomy 8:2
And thou shalt remember all the way which the LORD thy God led thee these forty years in the wilderness, to humble thee, and to prove thee, to know what was in thine heart, whether thou wouldest keep his commandments, or no.

Deuteronomy 8:3
And he humbled thee, and suffered thee to hunger, and fed thee with manna, which thou knewest not, neither did thy fathers know; that he might make thee know that man doth not live by bread only, but by every word that proceedeth out of the mouth of the LORD doth man live.

Deuteronomy 8:16
Who fed thee in the wilderness with manna, which thy fathers knew not, that he might humble thee, and that he might prove thee, to do thee good at thy latter end;

Deuteronomy 21:14
And it shall be, if thou have no delight in her, then thou shalt let her go whither she will; but thou shalt not sell her at all for money, thou shalt not make merchandise of her, because thou hast humbled her.

Deuteronomy 22:24

Then ye shall bring them both out unto the gate of that city, and ye shall stone them with stones that they die; the damsel, because she cried not, being in the city; and the man, because he hath humbled his neighbour's wife: so thou shalt put away evil from among you.

Deuteronomy 22:29

Then the man that lay with her shall give unto the damsel's father fifty shekels of silver, and she shall be his wife; because he hath humbled her, he may not put her away all his days.

Judges 19:24

Behold, here is my daughter a maiden, and his concubine; them I will bring out now, and humble ye them, and do with them what seemeth good unto you: but unto this man do not so vile a thing.

1 Kings 21:29

Seest thou how Ahab humbleth himself before me? because hehumbleth himself before me, I will not bring the evil in his days: but in his son's days will I bring the evil upon his house.

I [ahy]

I , possessive my or mine, objective me

used by a speaker in referring to himself or herself.

If I, I, I, I, I is the basis of all of your conversations?... Are you so self-absorbed where the world cannot seem to find its place into your world?
Life has its way of sending us through many different phases, and within each phase is a new level that we learn something different. With encounters of others we begin to learn more and more of how people function and how we handle ourselves with the differences of personalities. It's then we learn how the I remain true to the individual you aim to be. If you were asked to describe the I that you are, what would be your definition? Is it the I that knows it's purpose? Is it the I that understands it is about more than just you? Is it the I that exemplifies our heavenly Father and strives to give the best effort to enhance the land we live? Today, I encourage you to evaluate the I that you are.

INSECURITY \ˌin-si-ˈkyur\

not confident about yourself or your ability to do things well : nervous and uncomfortable
not certain to continue or be successful for a long time

INSECURITY is a poison that has the ability to destroy you. INSECURITIES lie within the deep core of our inner or outer beings. It controls our thoughts making us second guess about our place of acceptance in the atmospheric society in which we conduct our lives.

Commercialism has reduced so many to compare and compete. INSECURITIES will make you feel incomplete with overbearing self-doubt.

Losing the true value of self-worth has led so many to become materialistic and vain while teaching generations to accept mockery as normal behavior. We have begun crossing boundaries that should have never existed. People are worshiping idiotic idols putting God on the back burner and congratulating the devil's craftsmanship.

INSECURITIES that live within so many are fueling others to poke fun of the sick, the disabled, babies and even elderly while calling it all in "fun of humor"? To who? To those who will cry themselves to sleep at night because they were belittled and hackled by someone who only wanted a cheap laugh fest at the expense of others? Attempting to live by the rules governed by a lost society will leave you lost. Not knowing your greatness is rooted deep within.

You are the heir to the King that created the heavens and the earth. Build your self-worth on that principle alone.

Go confidently into the world and be an example of how wonderful it is to love yourself and others through the darkness while shedding the light.

INTEGRITY |inˈteɡritē|

the quality of being honest and having strong moral principles; moral uprightness : he is known to be a man of integrity.

One that can exemplify INTEGRITY is one that stands as an honest individual that holds firmly on their beliefs in the times of turmoil. Planting your feet firmly on the grounds of which you stand when others are persuading you to sway or stray away and do what they may feel is the general consensus to appease the masses. INTEGRITY should be more than what others recognize you by.
INTEGRITY should be amongst the marks you hold yourself accountable on when you think of yourself.
Be one of great character. One that has left such a stance of being on the up and up against all odds. Let your INTEGRITY speak on your behalf before your words are ever spoken.

Psalms 25:21
Let integrity and uprightness preserve me; for I wait on thee.

Psalms 78:72
So he fed them according to the integrity of his heart; and guided them by the skilfulness of his hands.

Proverbs 19:1
Better is the poor that walketh in his integrity, than he that is perverse in his lips, and is a fool.

Proverbs 20:7
The just man walketh in his integrity: his children are blessed after him.

Job 31:6
Let me be weighed in an even balance, that God may know mine integrity.

Psalms 26:11
But as for me, I will walk in mine integrity: redeem me, and be merciful unto me.

Psalms 41:12
And as for me, thou upholdest me in mine integrity, and settest me before thy face forever.

Proverbs 11:3
The integrity of the upright shall guide them: but the perverseness of transgressors shall destroy them.

Genesis 20:5
Said he not unto me, She is my sister? and she, even she herself said, He is my brother: in the integrity of my heart and innocency of my hands have I done this.

Job 2:9
Then said his wife unto him, Dost thou still retain thine integrity? curse God, and die.

Job 27:5

God forbid that I should justify you: till I die I will not remove mine integrity from me.

Psalms 7:8

The Lord shall judge the people: judge me, O Lord, according to my righteousness, and according to mine integrity that is in me.

INTELLIGENCE |inˈtelijəns|

the ability to acquire and apply knowledge and skills : an eminent man of great intelligence

INTELLIGENCE is not always based on the information you have, but the ability to use the information in your favor. Making INTELLIGENT decisions come with a level of maturity and a conscience effort. We must strive to be INTELLIGENT enough to recognize what is in our best interest and that which is not. Understanding how to be INTELLIGENT enough to know the difference between the time to speak and when to remain silent. Using our INTELLIGENCE to identify which has been sent as bait or as fate. Having all of the working pieces to a puzzle is only half of the equation, using the INTELLIGENCE to place the pieces of the puzzle in alignment to display the structure intended requires the effort of sorting through the pieces to reveal the vision.

JEALOUS | ˈjeləs |

feeling or showing envy of someone or their achievements and advantages
: he grew jealous of her success.

JEALOUSY has been the root of evil since the beginning of time. It has torn families apart, ripped leadership from the powerful and prevented empires from thriving due to callus and maliciousness towards one another.
JEALOUSY is one of the heaviest burdens one can bare. It will make you focus on the blessings of others while diminishing your own. We must learn to thrive and become successful individuals while respecting the importance of togetherness. To uplift others in their accomplishments and to encourage them to continue to inspire others to carry out greatness. A JEALOUS heart is filled with hostility and will only hinder you from reaching your next level of accomplishments. Search your heart over and pray for our sisters and brothers in Christ so that we can keep each other uplifted in His spirit.

JOY |joi|

a feeling of great pleasure and happiness : tears of joy | the joy of being alive.

JOY is the result of an inner peace found when you become at ease with yourself. JOY can be obtained once you free yourself of the burden of being acceptable in the eyes of a society that has limited your heights in comparison to their watered down version of your worth. JOY is the indescribable notion that allows you to overlook the obstacles that have come your way in attempts to hold you down. Releasing the bondage of the mental shackles that have held you from finding a feeling of worthiness will bring you onto the path of finding JOY.

1 Thessalonians 2:20
For ye are our glory and joy.

Acts 8:8
And there was great joy in that city.

1 Thessalonians 3:9
For what thanks can we render to God again for you, for all the joy wherewith we joy for your sakes before our God;

Esther 8:16
The Jews had light, and gladness, and joy, and honour.

Psalms 126:5
They that sow in tears shall reap in joy.

Jeremiah 49:25
How is the city of praise not left, the city of my joy!

Acts 13:52
And the disciples were filled with joy, and with the Holy Ghost.

Philippians 2:18
For the same cause also do ye joy, and rejoice with me.

Isaiah 9:3
Thou hast multiplied the nation, and not increased the joy: they joy before thee according to the joy in harvest, and as men rejoice when they divide the spoil.

Job 8:19
Behold, this is the joy of his way, and out of the earth shall others grow.

Job 20:5
That the triumphing of the wicked is short, and the joy of the hypocrite but for a moment?

Job 41:22
In his neck remaineth strength, and sorrow is turned into joy before him.

Psalms 35:9
And my soul shall be joyful in the Lord: it shall rejoice in his salvation.

KINDNESS |kahynd-nis|

kind deed
the quality or state of being kind

The golden rule, "do unto others as you would have them do unto you" is a coined phrase mentioned with the intent to remind you to treat others with the KINDESS that you would expect them to treat you with.
It is not as easy to attract a positive crowd if you are spewing angry or hurtful words into the atmosphere. During difficult and pleasant situations just the same you should put forth effort to control your temper and reflect a spirit of KINDNESS. Misunderstandings turn detrimental when gasoline is added to a flame. Bold actions driven by ANGER has led to far too many unfortunate situations that could have possibly been defused by KINDNESS or utilizing the ability to decide to turn the other cheek.
A firm hand is a stern hand is a general rule that is often misunderstood and power becomes abused.
Remember, eliminating the KINDNESS of the spirit of the Lord that can control and direct a situation better than an attitude of hostility can crumble and destroy what was meant to be nurtured and flourish.

Rule with the spirit of KINDESS.

Psalm 36:7
How precious is your loving kindness, O God! And the children of men take refuge in the shadow of your wings.

Psalm 117:2 - For His loving kindness is great toward us, and the truth of the Lord is everlasting.

Proverbs 11:25 - The generous person will be prosperous, and he who waters will himself be watered.

Proverbs 19:22 - What is desirable in a person is kindness, and it is better to be poor than a liar.

Matthew 6:21 - Where your treasure is, there will your heart be also.

Matthew 6:34a - Do not be anxious for tomorrow; tomorrow will care for itself.

Luke 6:27-31 - Love your enemies, do good to those who hate you, bless those who curse you, pray for those who mistreat you. If someone strikes you on one cheek, turn to him the other also. If someone takes your cloak, do not stop him from taking your tunic. Give to everyone who asks you, and if anyone takes what belongs to you, do not demand it back. Do to others as you would have them do to you.

Luke 6:36-38 - Be merciful, just as your Father is merciful. And do not judge and you will not be judged; and do not condemn, and you will not be condemned; pardon, and you will be pardoned. Give and it will be given to you; good measure, pressed down, shaken together, running over, they will pour into your lap. For by your standard of measure it will be measured to you in return.

Acts 20:35
It is more blessed to give than to receive.

I Corinthians 13:4-8
Love is patient, love is kind, and is not jealous; love does not brag and is not arrogant, does not act unbecomingly; it does not seek its own, is not provoked, does not take into account a wrong suffered, does not rejoice in unrighteousness, but rejoices with the truth. Love bears all things, believes all things, hopes all things, endures all things. Love never fails. Now abide faith, hope and love, these three; but the greatest of these is love.

Galatians 6:9
Let us not lose heart in doing good.

Ephesians 6:7
With good will render service, as to the Lord, and not to men.

Philippians 2:3-7
Do nothing from selfishness or empty conceit, but with humility of mind let each of you regard one another as more important than himself; do not merely look out for your own personal interests, but also for the interests of others. Have this attitude in yourselves which was also in Christ Jesus, who, although He existed in the form of God, did not regard equality with God a thing to be grasped, but emptied Himself, taking the form of a bond-servant, and being made in the likeness of men.

Philippians 4:4-8

Rejoice in the Lord always; again I will say, rejoice! Let your forbearing spirit be known to all men. The Lord is near. Be anxious for nothing, but in everything by prayer and supplication with thanksgiving let your requests be made known to God. And the peace of God, which surpasses all comprehension, shall guard your hearts and minds in Christ Jesus. Finally, brethren, whatever is true, whatever is honorable, whatever is right, whatever is pure, whatever is lovely, whatever is of good repute, if there is any excellence and if anything worthy of praise, let your mind dwell on these things.

I John 3:19

We love, because He first loved us.

Hebrews 13:1-2

Let love of the brethren continue. Do not neglect to show hospitality to strangers, for by this some have entertained angels without knowing it.

James 3:17-18

For where jealousy and selfish ambition exist, there is disorder and every evil thing. But the wisdom from above is first pure, then peaceable, reasonable, full of mercy and good fruits, unwavering, without hypocrisy. And the seed whose fruit is righteousness is sown in peace by those who make peace.

KINDRED \ˈkin-drəd\

Family ties to the source of your existence.
a group of related individuals

KINDRED, that of your kind. KINDRED, heirs of the same lineage. KINDRED, family ties to the source of your existence. Closely related or distant we are of KINDRED souls through our heavenly Father. We were made in His image and are all sister and brothers in Christ. With the family morals of being KIND to one another and looking out for others in their time of need brings us closer to the intended purpose of spreading the love that God has exemplified.

Numbers 10:30
And he said unto him, I will not go; but I will depart to mine own land, and to my kindred.

1 Chronicles 16:28
Give unto the Lord, ye kindreds of the people, give unto the Lord glory and strength.

Esther 2:10
Esther had not shewed her people nor her kindred: for Mordecai had charged her that she should not shew it.

Luke 1:61
And they said unto her, There is none of thy kindred that is called by this name.

Acts 7:14
Then sent Joseph, and called his father Jacob to him, and all his kindred, threescore and fifteen souls.

Genesis 24:4
But thou shalt go unto my country, and to my kindred, and take a wife unto my son Isaac.

Genesis 24:38
But thou shalt go unto my father's house, and to my kindred, and take a wife unto my son.

Genesis 24:41
Then shalt thou be clear from this my oath, when thou comest to my kindred; and if they give not thee one, thou shalt be clear from my oath.

LOVE |ləv|

a great interest and pleasure in something : his love for football | we share a love of music.

LOVE has different meanings to us all. There are so many ways to express or display LOVE but none greater than that presented to us every day by our heavenly Father. Agape LOVE a "selfless LOVE".
Looking at the conditions of the world today, to give LOVE or to be LOVED does not seem to be such a priority as it had been yonder years ago. The ultimate expression of them all :"For God so loved the world that he gave His only begotten SON. John 3:16".
It takes compassion to move a person to give of themselves towards the betterment of another.
Compromise is key in LOVE.

LOVE.. a word that has so many definitions and can be summed up by the verse John 3:16 which exemplifies the act of what LOVE truly is. The action of giving of yourself, your prized possession or even placing yourself in an uncomfortable state for the benefit of another.
For God so loved the world that He gave his only begotten Son. John 3:16
God loved us so much He made the ultimate sacrifice of His Son, Jesus Christ to save all who confess with their mouths and believe in their hearts that because of the LOVE the Lord made known for us that we have access to life everlasting.

Luke 6:32
For if ye love them which love you, what thank have ye? for sinners also love those that love them.

1 John 4:19
We love him, because he first loved us.

1 Samuel 20:17
And Jonathan caused David to swear again, because he loved him: for he loved him as he loved his own soul.

John 15:9
As the Father hath loved me, so have I loved you: continue ye in my love.

1 John 4:10
Herein is love, not that we loved God, but that he loved us, and sent his Son to be the propitiation for our sins.

John 15:12
This is my commandment, That ye love one another, as I have loved you.

John 14:15
If ye love me, keep my commandments.

1 Corinthians 16:24
My love be with you all in Christ Jesus. Amen.

Hebrews 13:1
Let brotherly love continue.

Genesis 25:28
And Isaac loved Esau, because he did eat of his venison: but Rebekah loved Jacob.

Proverbs 8:17
I love them that love me; and those that seek me early shall find me.

LOYALTY loy·al·ty

a feeling of faithfulness or allegiance
Faithfulness or devotion to a person, a cause,
obligations, or duties

LOYALTY, an understanding that can be quite difficult to categorize as the basis of it may waiver due to the circumstances it was formed.
LOYALTY has been tossed into the flame of convenience for so long it is harder to measure its truth.
Misplaced LOYALTY that has faltered our outlook on what LOYALTY is, has made us struggle with recognizing the true example. Causing us to believe no one is capable of being upright with their words and expecting them to move unsteadily. Perhaps being LOYAL to disloyal people has jilted your perspective on how LOYALTY is displayed in our lives daily.
Do not let the negligence of mankind taint the LOYALTY you have been blessed with.
The Lord has been LOYAL to His word since the beginning of time. He stated to be with us always.

Isaiah 41:10
So do not fear, for I am with you; do not be dismayed, for I am your God. I will strengthen you with my righteous right hand.

Matthew 28:20
Teaching them to observe all things whatsoever I have commanded you. And lo, I am with you always, even until the end of the world.
Amen

LOYALTY seals the trust. LOYALTY is not routine. It adjusts while holding steadfast even during trials and tribulations. LOYALTY is a bond that compels you to give your all every time in every situation to solidify a united force to be reckoned. The LOYALTY of Christ to fulfill His obligation unto the kingdom is an example to recall every day of your life. Even when the clouds were low and the burden was heavy, He never swayed from the path. Although LOYALTY may not come from those we may expect or desire it, we should remain LOYAL to Christ on our mission of doing the Lord's work. Prioritizing where you place your LOYALTY determines your unspoken truth. Where does your LOYALTY stand?

LUST ləst|
very strong sexual desire
: he knew that his lust for her had returned.

The spirit of LUST. The longing desire and burning temptation of LUST can be a dangerous thing. Emotions are provoked by many gateways. It is very important that we monitor the relationships we nurture. LUST can strike anyone at any given time in many forms and usually when you least expect. Attractions strike and alerts your curiosity. The pure thoughts become tainted with questions of "what ifs?" and "what could it hurt?" or "what if no one ever found out?" Truth of the matter is if you decided to carry out the actions and never breathed a word to another living soul, God never blinks. Add the question of "Is it worth it?" to your list before thrusting yourself into a situation that may lead to a line of regret.
It is the LUSTING spirit that has played the role of so many unhappy relationships. Relationships of husband and wife, coworkers, friends and strangers are affected by it every day. It becomes difficult to return to a less stressful state of being after adding fuel to a flame. LUSTING or desiring the company of another while being attached to someone has so many unnecessary complications that hindsight unravels and makes play by play narration loud and clear. Pray for wisdom to know the outcome of LUST may not be worth the thrills of falling into the trap. Ask God to grant you the strength to fight through the LUSTING spirit and deliver you with a clear conscience.

1 Corinthians 10:6
Now these things were our examples, to the intent we should not lust after evil things, as they also lusted.

1 John 2:16
For all that is in the world, the lust of the flesh, and the lust of the eyes, and the pride of life, is not of the Father, but is of the world.

Psalms 78:30
They were not estranged from their lust. But while their meat was yet in their mouths,

Galatians 5:24
And they that are Christ's have crucified the flesh with the affections and lusts.

Psalms 78:18
And they tempted God in their heart by asking meat for their lust.

Psalms 81:12
So I gave them up unto their own hearts' lust: and they walked in their own counsels.

Psalms 106:14
But lusted exceedingly in the wilderness, and tempted God in the desert.

1 Thessalonians 4:5
Not in the lust of concupiscence, even as the Gentiles which know not God:

James 1:14
But every man is tempted, when he is drawn away of his own lust, and enticed.

1 Peter 1:14
As obedient children, not fashioning yourselves according to the former lusts in your ignorance:

Jude 1:18
How that they told you there should be mockers in the last time, who should walk after their own ungodly lusts.

MISERY | ˈmiz(ə)rē |

a state or feeling of great distress or discomfort of mind or body : she went upstairs and cried in misery | he wrote endlessly about his frustrations and miseries.

MISERY loves company.... But why? If MISERY is such a tough emotion why are we so quick to drag another into the pit of distress with us? There are many factors that can factor into our unhappiness. Many of which we can control or even avoid with skillful and proactive thinking. The grief that comes along with some of the decisions we make with the pity parties to follow is a vicious cycle. MISERY can lead to deadly thoughts and dreadful actions. Being in such a slump it becomes difficult to see things clearly and the light at the end of the tunnel grows dim and begin to fade. Where there is a mindset of hopelessness, panic and fear are lurking leading you to a desperate situation and it's no secret that desperate people do desperate things. Covering our tracks and not facing the problem is only adding fuel to the fire and deepens the MISERY.

Romans 3:16
Destruction and misery are in their ways:

Proverbs 31:7
Let him drink, and forget his poverty, and remember his misery no more.

Lamentations 3:19
Remembering mine affliction and my misery, the wormwood and the gall.

Job 3:20
Wherefore is light given to him that is in misery, and life unto the bitter in soul;

Job 11:16
Because thou shalt forget thy misery, and remember it as waters that pass away:

Ecclesiastes 8:6
Because to every purpose there is time and judgment, therefore the misery of man is great upon him.

Judges 10:16
And they put away the strange gods from among them, and served the Lord: and his soul was grieved for the misery of Israel.

James 5:1
Go to now, ye rich men, weep and howl for your miseries that shall come upon you.

Lamentations 1:7
Jerusalem remembered in the days of her affliction and of her miseries all her pleasant things that she had in the days of old, when her people fell into the hand of the enemy, and none did help her: the adversaries saw her, and did mock at her sabbaths.

MODEST | ˈmädəst |

unassuming or moderate in the estimation of one's abilities or achievements
: he was a very modest man, refusing to take any credit for the enterprise.

MODESTY a humbling attitude that speaks volumes of a person's character. A boastful spirit is a prideful persona that may show an arrogance of achievement that does not belong to one in the first place. All blessings are received from our Heavenly Father. Meaning He is to be glorified in all of our ways and acknowledgments. A meek and mild manner of reaching goals or obtaining objects and rewards are to be done so in a way which we show our gratitude more so then show our self-puff as if we did it on our own. The Lord maintained a MODEST spirit and we should follow His lead.

1 Timothy 2:9 (KJV)
In like manner also, that women adorn themselves in modest apparel, with shamefacedness and sobriety; not with broided hair, or gold, or pearls, or costly array;

MURDER | ˈmərdər |

The unlawful premeditated killing of one human being by another
: he was put on trial for attempted murder.

MURDER in our community has become nearly common as breathing. The total disregard for human life has the world desensitized and completely detached from saving a life rather than taking one. Anger and rage is lurking in the souls of those who are not armed with the word and spiritual warfare becomes physical. The glorification of MURDER lives through the sources that remains a part of a daily routine. The things that enters the spirit consciously and subconsciously can feed the soul and whisper unhealthy ingredients that leads to destruction.
The first recorded MURDER in the Bible took place between two brothers. The story of Kane and Abel was many years ago and only shows that there is nothing new under the sun. Jealousy, anger, hatred are all factors that adds fuel to a fire that is burning out of control. MURDER is forbidden by the ten commandments. Life is not ours to give nor take. MURDER is an act that is irreversible. Once the act is committed, there are no do overs, second chances or even apologies that will alleviate the pain and destruction that has been caused. The decision of taking a life is one that comes with many consequences and should not be taken lightly. Our jails are to capacity and grave yards are filling quickly with a life that has been taken by the wrath of MURDER.

The day we can begin to respect each other and take the value of being my brother's keeper to heart, is the day we will become closer to ending a MURDEROUS streak amongst our loved ones.

Numbers 35:16
And if he smite him with an instrument of iron, so that he die, he is a murderer: the murderer shall surely be put to death.

Psalms 94:6
They slay the widow and the stranger, and murder the fatherless.

Revelation 9:21
Neither repented they of their murders, nor of their sorceries, nor of their fornication, nor of their thefts.

Numbers 35:17
And if he smite him with throwing a stone, wherewith he may die, and he die, he is a murderer: the murderer shall surely be put to death.

Numbers 35:18
Or if he smite him with an hand weapon of wood, wherewith he may die, and he die, he is a murderer: the murderer shall surely be put to death.

1 John 3:15
Whosoever hateth his brother is a murderer: and ye know that no murderer hath eternal life abiding in him.

Numbers 35:19
The revenger of blood himself shall slay the murderer: when he meeteth him, he shall slay him.

Job 24:14
The murderer rising with the light killeth the poor and needy, and in the night is as a thief.

Mark 7:21
For from within, out of the heart of men, proceed evil thoughts, adulteries, fornications, murders,

NO |nō|
not any
: there is no excuse

NO should not be an option when it comes to pursuing and achieving your goals. NO is a word that has struck fear into so many potential leaders and have frozen stiff the flame of what was once a burning desire of a trailblazer that may have never put forth the energy because of being limited by hearing a NO. At times, God may answer us with a NO. Not to discourage us, but to prepare us and mature us to the place He will have us before allowing us to hear otherwise from Him.

Recognizing the power of NO is also important. Knowing that you are accountable for the decisions you make sometimes you will have to stand firm and say NO.

NO to compromising your worth to conform to a route that may not best suit the vision of your GOALS. Knowing to say NO to peer pressure that will lead you down the path away from your preferred destination. Saying NO to temptations that are presented is an example of strength and will power that will build your character and bring you closer to your purpose.

NOW [nou]

at the present time or moment
: You are now using a dictionary.

NOW is the time for us to begin putting our best foot forward. NOW is the time to step into our dreams. NOW is the time for us to emerge from a painful past and build a brilliant future. We often spend too much time dwelling on the past. Not allowing ourselves to focus on NOW which will build a bridge to our next step of which is to come. "Then" has become a crutch that mentally binds us. Giving too much thought to what happened then and why we feel as if we cannot readjust NOW. We serve a right NOW God. Knowing that God is with us in the NOW should be all of the reassurance we need in order to put our best foot forward.

A scripture that depicts the strength of NOW is

Hebrews 11:1
"Now faith is the substance of things hoped for, the evidence of things not seen."

It states that NOW faith, is the substance….
Implement FAITH NOW as the SUBSTANCE which will be the basis of your efforts. Make your NOW count. Do not ALLOW your hands to become idle and used as the devil's workshop. Today is the NOW that can make the difference in your tomorrow. Act NOW.

OPTION [op-shuh n]

the power or right of choosing.
something that may be or is chosen; choice.

Granted we have the OPTION to make choices of our own free will, the responsibility of doing that which is right is solely on us.
OPTIONS are always available in every aspect of our life. Being that OPTIONS are available we must decide which OPTION is best for us. Just because we have OPTIONS on hand, it is not always in our best interest to explore them all.
Weighing OPTIONS and the outcome which each are accompanied by is one of the greatest weaknesses displayed. Are the OPTIONS we chose aligned with the outcome we anticipate for our vision? We have the OPTION to try or to give up. We have the OPTION to love or to hate. We have the OPTION to shape our world in a positive or a negative way. Let your OPTIONS speak volumes on your character.

OPTIMISTIC äptə'mistik

hopeful and confident about the future

Focus on becoming more OPTIMISTIC. The way you see the outline is how you will paint the picture.
Convince yourself daily that you are starting your day on the good foot and ending on a high note. You set the tone stemming from the very first string of events in your day, leading into every turn of events that come your way and ultimately the outcome. Roll through life with a level of expectation that the best is yet to come. There are many unexpected situations that the enemy will throw in your path to shake you and attempt to bend your faith.
Do not give it the authority to change your belief.
Know that what the devil meant for bad… God will use for your good. See the highlight of the rainbow across the sky by looking beyond the grey clouds. Think of the rain as liquid sunshine. Begin to see every obstacle as an option to learn and grow and not as a hindrance or a setback. Today is your day to see the world through the vision God has bestowed upon you and not through the sight that the world has dictated to you. Be the example of the change you desire to see in the kingdom by doing the Lord's work. Being optimistic is a sign of your faith. Troubles won't last always… the atmosphere is shifting and He is working it out for you.

OPPORTUNITY äpər't(y)oonədē

a set of circumstances that makes it possible to do something

OPPORTUNITY is the presentation of many things, be it large or small, good or bad. Every day that you are granted here on earth is yet another OPPORTUNITY to right your wrongs or even create your mark on your legacy.
The possibilities are only limited by the amount of energy you place into them. Are you waiting on OPPORTUNITIES or making them? Knowing what you would like to accomplish gives you an edge. You have an idea of what steps you should take towards your dreams. Being prepared sets you apart from landing an OPPORTUNITY or missing one. There is one important fact we should remember… OPPORTUNITIES will expose the truth we sometimes forget to tell. We can say how bad we want just that one chance to make it to the next level, but when the time comes and we are standing face to face with the set of circumstances that could make it possible we show our level of commitment to the dream that has finally showed up to see us.
When OPPORTUNITY knocks will you rise to the occasion or run from the chance that could have possibly been sent to help you fulfill your purpose?
Today, spend time writing your plan. Make it clear. What is the next step towards that direction? What OPPORTUNITIES would you like to come your way? Align your vision with your actions.
Today has granted you that OPPORTUNITY.

PATIENCE | ˈpā sh əns |

the capacity to accept or tolerate delay, trouble, or suffering without getting angry or upset

: you can find bargains if you have the patience to sift through the dross.

PATIENCE is kind, loving and calm. Like what God has for us.

Isaiah 40:31 KJV

"But they that wait upon the Lord shall renew their strength; they shall mount up with wings as eagles; they shall run, and not be weary; and they shall walk, and not faint."

Wanting to move before He grants us permission or points us in which way we should go due to us being restless in our PATIENCE with God, can lead us to run in a direction of destruction.
Losing our PATIENCE and giving in to the devil's urges to test God's will for us will knock us another blow.
What if God began to lose His PATIENCE with us?
If God were to turn His back on us the instant we decided not to do as He said?
Would that be the moment we realized the true importance of PATIENCE?
Going through situations that requires you to work through with your PATIENCE is not a pit of defeat, but a time to Accept the lessons that are being taught. Being still in the spiritual when the physical may be anxious to run away.

Leaning on the word that was left to encourage you during the times you feel as if the motions are leading you to another dead end. Go to your quiet place, seek peace as you pray for the PATIENCE to not only stand but to pass the test. Do not attempt to rush God's plans for you. He is never early, never late, but always right on time. Be PATIENT and trust in Him.

PEACE pēs/

freedom from disturbance; quiet and tranquility.

"you can while away an hour or two in peace and seclusion"

In troubled times we search for a piece of PEACE.
The calm in the midst of the storm. A quiet place that we can gather our thoughts, weigh our options and pray for guidance.
With so many uncertainties that occur within our lives our stress levels peak and shake like a leaf on a tree as the wind blows. The world spins and situations dwindle from our grasp and we become frantic. In a panic state of mind we tend to react differently than we would with a composed mind set. The disturbances within our space throws the urgencies in our face and we lose track of this being a test. A restless mind will keep you up at night tossing and turning unable to find PEACE. A heart broken by a vision of love will leave you confused on when or how to love again until you have mended it with PEACE.
No matter what is going on in your life right now, remember that Jesus has already commanded it to be still, allowing PEACE to be with you.

Mark 4:39
And he awoke and rebuked the wind and said to the sea, "Peace! Be still!" And the wind ceased, and there was a great calm.

Psalm 29:11 NIV
The LORD gives strength to his people; the LORD blesses his people with peace.

Psalm 34:14
Turn from evil and do good; seek peace and pursue it.

Psalm 37:37
Consider the blameless, observe the upright; a future awaits those who seek peace.

Psalm 85:8
I will listen to what God the LORD says; he promises peace to his people, his faithful servants— but let them not turn to folly.

Psalm 119:165
Great peace have those who love your law, and nothing can make them stumble.

Isaiah 9:6
For to us a child is born, to us a son is given, and the government will be on his shoulders. And he will be called Wonderful Counselor, Mighty God, Everlasting Father, Prince of Peace.

Isaiah 26:3
You will keep in perfect peace those whose minds are steadfast, because they trust in you.

Isaiah 26:12
LORD, you establish peace for us; all that we have accomplished you have done for us.

Isaiah 54:10
Though the mountains be shaken and the hills be removed, yet my unfailing love for you will not be shaken nor my covenant of peace be removed," says the LORD, who has compassion on you.

Isaiah 55:12
You will go out in joy and be led forth in peace; the mountains and hills will burst into song before you, and all the trees of the field will clap their hands.

John 14:27
Peace I leave with you; my peace I give you. I do not give to you as the world gives. Do not let your hearts be troubled and do not be afraid.

PREPARATION [prep-uh-rey-shuh n]

any proceeding, experience, or the like considered as a mode of preparing for the future.

Always remember the 5 P's :
Prior **P**REPARATION **p**revents **p**oor **p**erformance! The amount of effort you put in today will dictate the amount of effort tomorrow will give you. Looking forward to being presented new opportunities is great. Opportunities being presented to you when you are not ready can be a discouragement. Putting forth the effort before the due date is the PREPARATION that will set you a place above or a step behind. How PREPARED are you to weather the storm of life? There are conditions that come with or without warning. High beams may cause for sunscreen, while hard rain calls for umbrellas. The smooth sailing will allow you to travel the beautiful sea but are you PREPARED for the waves once you leave the shore? God wants us to be PREPARED and rooted in His word. The enemy is lurking and awaiting the right time to catch you off guard and if you are not PREPARED the feat will be done with ease. PREPARE yourself every day by finding the tools needed in your conversations with Christ. PREPARE yourself to be a champion by giving your best before the test, so that when the day comes you have studied hard and will be PREPARED.

PURPOSE | ˈpərpəs |

the reason for which something is done or created or for which something exists
: the purpose of the meeting is to appoint a trustee

Just as we were born into the world, we were born into our PURPOSE. God makes no mistakes. Before you filled your lungs with the first breath of air, God had already assigned a PURPOSE on our life.

Your PURPOSE becomes clearer as you begin to allow Christ to be the captain of your soul. Leading a PURPOSE driven life is aligned when our steps are ordered by God. We enter into seasons not knowing what to expect upon our arrival, but once the veil is lifted from our eyes we begin to understand more by and by.

Family, friends, relationships, colleagues, strangers.... anyone that you interact with all serve a PURPOSE in your life just as you serve a PURPOSE in theirs.

The mark you leave along this trail of life as you travel through is a part of your PURPOSE. Pray and ask for clarity as you long to fill your PURPOSE to the best of your abilities.

May your tongue stem with the PURPOSE to uplift your brethren.

May your actions display PURPOSE of love for your neighbor.

May your daily walk with Christ lead YOU to living to the highest potential of your PURPOSE.

QUESTION 'kwesCH(ə)n/

a sentence worded or expressed so as to elicit information

Who? What? When? Where? Why?
Five basic yet very essential QUESTIONS.

Who are you?
What are your goals?
When do you plan on getting started?
Where do you see this going?
Why is it worth it?

Who sent you?
What is your purpose?
When did you decide to take this journey?
Where is your faith?
Why should I believe you?

Who inspires you?
What motivates you?
When did you first see the light?
Where do you seek guidance?
Why have our paths crossed?

Without asking QUESTIONS we won't find the answers. Without being honest within our quest we will find it difficult to come to a conclusion built on a solid foundation. At times we shy away from asking certain QUESTIONS that we know the answers may sway our decisions.

Have you ever found yourself avoiding a series of QUESTIONS that you might be asked in return?

Was there ever a time you avoided asking a QUESTION because you knew the truth would require something more of you? Is it easier for you just to say "I didn't know?"

Are you willing to face your fear of the unknown and search for answers? There is a sense of peace in knowing. Is this the right thing to do? Would God be pleased with my choice? Am I ready to take full responsibility or even face the consequences? Who else will be affected by the outcome? Is the risk worth the effort? Have I spent enough time in prayer? Am I leaving the mark of excellence or are we settling for mediocracy? Does my desire reflect my sacrifice? Is it of Christ? Have you encouraged someone today along the way? Have you told anyone about the goodness of the Lord? Are you obeying the word and seeking the kingdom first in all of your endeavors? QUESTIONS that will help us dig deeper as we are searching for growth. Ask God to give you the answers that you need in order to lead a life pleasing in His sight.

QUIET ˈkwīət/

making little or no noise.

Beware of the QUIET storms brewing in your life. It won't always be the loud, long awaited announcements that will show up on your doorstep. Sometimes the QUIET battles are the strongest.
QUIET your mind. The distractions that find you while you are seeking answers to guide you in the direction you should go could possibly altar your destination.
So many things are becoming a part of the soundtrack of our lives that we forget the power of silence.
It wasn't until I sat in my QUIET place, removed from all distractions of others, phones, televisions and alerts that I was able to hear a word from God.
When was the last time you visited your QUIET place to meditate, pray and gather your thoughts? Clear the clutter, remove the distractions and focus on what message the Holy Spirit is delivering to you in that QUIET, still voice. Find the answers that will place you on solid ground.

QUIT kwit/

leave (a place), usually permanently

We have been told time and time again to "never QUIT". In all actuality, sometimes QUITTING is the very thing we should be doing.

QUIT making excuses for why we are not doing the things that need to be done in order to get it done.

QUIT responding to negativity. Learn to KNOW when to walk away from situations that are not conducive to painting the bigger picture.

QUIT doing the work of the devil and expecting God to bless our mess.

QUIT serving two masters, running in circles of sheep and wolves and not being decisive in our decisions.

QUIT comparing your situation to others…
You don't know the ins and outs of their story to glory.

QUIT compromising your morals to gain worldly attention while chipping away at the kingdom's representation.

QUIT complaining about every obstacle that comes your way. It is another opportunity to get closer to Christ.

QUIT stressing over temporary circumstances that God has told you He has already fixed.

QUIT avoiding the word when it is condemning your actions. Run to the word and find your PEACE.

QUIT belittling others to uplift yourself.

QUIT nurturing relationships that are nipping away at your soul.

QUIT being afraid to step out on FAITH.

QUIT allowing others to dictate your worth.

QUIT speaking negativity over your life. Spewing it into the atmosphere is only setting the shift in your direction.

QUIT hiding from the better version of yourself and put in the work to bring it to light.

QUIT thinking that no one is on your side and understand that God has your back.

QUIT waiting on a crisis before you kneel to pray. God is longing to hear from you today.

RESPECT rə'spekt/

a feeling of deep admiration for someone or something elicited by their abilities, qualities, or achievements.

There is a formula of three R's that I base my day around.

1. RESPECT for God.

2. RESPECT for self.

3. RESPECT for others.

RESPECT is something we all deserve.
RESPECT for God understanding that as children of God we owe our heavenly Father the utmost admiration.
We can never repay Him for all of the things that He has done for us, but we can honor Him by always keeping Him first.
RESPECT for self: Knowing who we are and who's we are validates us as an heir to all of the blessings one can ask.
RESPECTING the fact that we are royalty we are expected to carry ourselves of a certain stature.
The way we conduct ourselves speaks a louder volume than our words.
The RESPECT we expect from others should be displayed in the way we RESPECT ourselves.
RESPECT for others: If we are to love our neighbors as we love ourselves, then it is without a doubt we should show the RESPECT we would like to be shown to us.
RESPECTING others as they are one of God's children shows the RESPECT we have for Him.

Matthew 25:40 KJV

And the King shall answer and say unto them, Verily I say unto you, Inasmuch as ye have done it unto one of the least of these my brethren, ye have done it unto me.

REVELATION \ ˌre-və-ˈlā-shən\

a usually secret or surprising fact that is made known

This is the season we need to quit asking God to give us a REVELATION and then turn a blind eye to it and carry on as if He has not shown us the truth.
God grants us the REVELATION we seek when we pray and diligently seek Him. Fasting and praying asking God to make us more like Him as we decrease and as He increase.
I have found in asking God for REVELATION in many areas of my life, I failed to ask for the strength it would take in order for me to deal with what He REVEALED.
The people that are closest in your circle or maybe even your next of kin could possibly be the ones the Lord will show you through a different point of view.
REVELATIONS of that relationship you have been questioning for so long, not being what God has in store for you…..
REVELATIONS that you must let go of the things you have grown accustomed to…
REVELATIONS of beginning a new thing in order to be blessed with the best which is to come….
REVELATION that now is the time for you to bury your fear and self-doubt and step out on faith.
The REVELATION can cause turmoil within understanding seasons in the spiritual realm that God has shown us to release what we may desire in the physical.
Obedience will elevate us within the revelation.
Conviction in REVELATION requires right now attention.

Now that you know better, change is required and we are not to twiddle our thumbs or linger with the process.

God has revealed what is, in order for us to see what is to come. Trust and believe that He will never leave nor forsake you. While you are going through the transition and the roads may appear dark, there is a light at the end of the tunnel. Walk by faith and not by sight.

RULE rool/

one of a set of explicit or understood regulations or principles governing conduct within a particular activity or sphere.

RULES are set in place to moderate our conduct. A set of guidelines of acceptable and unacceptable behavior at a given time.

RULES that we chose to follow exposes the intent of our reasoning. There are RULES we have been given by parents, teachers, employers that we are expected to adhere to.

What about the RULES that were given to us by our heavenly Father?

The Ten Commandments

1. You shall have no other gods before Me.
2. You shall not make idols.
3. You shall not take the name of the LORD your God in vain.
4. Remember the Sabbath day, to keep it holy.
5. Honor your father and your mother.
6. You shall not murder.
7. You shall not commit adultery.
8. You shall not steal.
9. You shall not bear false witness against your neighbor.
10. You shall not covet.

The rules were so important as a guide for us that they were given more than once:

Exodus 20:2-17

1. *"I am the LORD your God, who brought you out of the land of Egypt, out of the house of bondage. You shall have no other gods before Me.*

2. *"You shall not make for yourself a carved image—any likeness of anything that is in heaven above, or that is in the earth beneath, or that is in the water under the earth; you shall not bow down to them nor serve them. For I, the LORD your God, am a jealous God, visiting the iniquity of the fathers upon the children to the third and fourth generations of those who hate Me, but showing mercy to thousands, to those who love Me and keep My commandments.*

3. *"You shall not take the name of the LORD your God in vain, for the LORD will not hold him guiltless who takes His name in vain.*

4. *"Remember the Sabbath day, to keep it holy. Six days you shall labor and do all your work, but the seventh day is the Sabbath of the LORD your God. In it you shall do no work: you, nor your son, nor your daughter, nor your male servant, nor your female servant, nor your cattle, nor your stranger who is within your gates. For in six days the LORD made the heavens and the earth, the sea, and all that is in them, and rested the seventh day. Therefore the LORD blessed the Sabbath day and hallowed it.*

5. *"Honor your father and your mother, that your days may be long upon the land which the LORD your God is giving you.*

6. *"You shall not murder.*

7. *"You shall not commit adultery.*

8. *"You shall not steal.*

9. *"You shall not bear false witness against your neighbor.*

10. *"You shall not covet your neighbor's house; you shall not covet your neighbor's wife, nor his male servant, nor his female servant,*

nor his ox, nor his donkey, nor anything that is your neighbor's."

Deuteronomy 5:6-21

1. *"I am the LORD your God who brought you out of the land of Egypt, out of the house of bondage. You shall have no other gods before Me.*

2. *"You shall not make for yourself a carved image—any likeness of anything that is in heaven above, or that is in the earth beneath, or that is in the water under the earth; you shall not bow down to them nor serve them. For I, the LORD your God, am a jealous God, visiting the iniquity of the fathers upon the children to the third and fourth generations of those who hate Me, but showing mercy to thousands, to those who love Me and keep My commandments.*

3. *"You shall not take the name of the LORD your God in vain, for the LORD will not hold him guiltless who takes His name in vain.*

4. *"Observe the Sabbath day, to keep it holy, as the LORD your God commanded you. Six days you shall labor and do all your work, but the seventh day is the Sabbath of the LORD your God. In it you shall do no work: you, nor your son, nor your daughter, nor your male servant, nor your female servant, nor your ox, nor your donkey, nor any of your cattle, nor your stranger who is within your gates, that your male servant and your female servant may rest as well as you. And remember that you were a slave in the land of Egypt, and the LORD your God brought you out from there by a mighty hand and by an outstretched arm; therefore the LORD your God commanded you to keep the Sabbath day.*

5. *"Honor your father and your mother, as the LORD your God has commanded you, that your days may be long, and that it may be well with you in the land which the LORD your God is giving you.*

6. *"You shall not murder.*

7. *"You shall not commit adultery.*

8. *"You shall not steal.*

9.   "You shall not bear false witness against your neighbor.
10.   "You shall not covet your neighbor's wife; and you shall not desire your neighbor's house, his field, his male servant, his female servant, his ox, his donkey, or anything that is your neighbor's."

The guidelines and level of expectation has been set and sent. Take note and hold the instructions closely as we go through this journey of life.

SACRIFICE ˈsakrəˌfīs/

an act of slaughtering an animal or person or surrendering a possession as an offering to God or to a divine or supernatural figure.

Has your SACRIFICE matched or exceeded your desires to be met?
We have the tendency to grow our expectations while expecting to avoid the required SACRIFICE to show ourselves worthy. Who are we to short change God by negotiating what we should be able to keep while demanding Him to give us more? If we are not taking inventory of our lives, we may be SACRIFICING valuable time that we cannot get back.
We may be SACRIFICING our morals for a streak of acceptance from the world. SACRIFICES are made daily... It is the balance of the give and take measure we end up in a tug-a-war with.
SACRIFICE is not just about the ability to give.
It is the ability to give beyond your normal realm of comfort.

"I've found SACRIFICE as the art of giving of your best and not what is just left of the rest." – LaTangela Sherman

SACRIFICE today for what you trust and believe God for tomorrow. When God gave us the ultimate SACRIFICE, He displayed such love.

JOHN 3:16
For God so loved the world that he gave his one and only Son, that whoever believes in him shall not perish but have eternal life.

Matthew 19:21
Jesus said to him, "If you wish to be complete, go and sell your possessions and give to the poor, and you will have treasure in heaven; and come, follow Me."

Luke 14:33
"So then, none of you can be My disciple who does not give up all his own possessions.

Luke 5:27-28
After that He went out and noticed a tax collector named Levi sitting in the tax booth, and He said to him, "Follow Me." And he left everything behind, and got up and began to follow Him.

Luke 22:42
saying, "Father, if You are willing, remove this cup from Me; yet not My will, but Yours be done."

STRUGGLE ˈstrəgəl/

make forceful or violent efforts to get free of restraint or constriction

What is your biggest STRUGGLE?
With so many temptations aiming for you, how do you manage to shake free and steer clear? Is it a STRUGGLE to find your way to the high road when someone has attempted to knock you down?
Have you ever found yourself wrestling with the "should I" or "should I not" decisions in life?
STRUGGLES in our spiritual, is a sign of growth.
Having to even weigh in on what is right and what is wrong is identifying that the Holy Spirit is talking to us as we are going through.
Whispering the consequences that we will be facing or the reward we are reaping.
Some may STRUGGLE with addictions to substances and some may STRUGGLE with being bold enough to leave a place of familiarity to seek the unknown heights awaiting us.
My STRUGGLE may be different than yours.
Your STRUGGLE may be different than mine.
We all face times where we may STRUGGLE to get from one level to the next. Never feel as if there is a point in life where the STRUGGLE aspect fades. Challenges come and our ABILITY to overcome them is possible.

REMINDER:

This STRUGGLE won't last and this too shall come to pass.

SUBMISSIVE səb'misiv/

ready to conform to the authority or will of others; meekly obedient or passive.

Before we become so willing to allow another to lead us, let us ask, " who have they SUBMITTED their will to?" Putting down your guard can be quite difficult. We bear more hurt than we probably care to admit and subjecting ourselves to being a moving target to earning another strike is not typically ideal.
Strong- willed, determined, relentless, the world has callused us so, we begin to see through a tarnished perspective.
Focus on the examples Christ left for the body to follow on SUBMISSION.

Job 22:21
"Yield now and be at peace with Him; Thereby good will come to you.

1 Peter 5:6
Therefore humble yourselves under the mighty hand of God, that He may exalt you at the proper time,

Psalm 2:9-11
'You shall break them with a rod of iron, You shall shatter them like earthenware.'" Now therefore, O kings, show discernment; Take warning, O judges of the earth. Worship the LORD with reverence And rejoice with trembling.

Matthew 6:9-10
"Pray, then, in this way: 'Our Father who is in heaven, Hallowed be Your name. 'Your kingdom come Your will be done, On earth as it is in heaven.

Hebrews 12:9
Furthermore, we had earthly fathers to discipline us, and we respected them; shall we not much rather be subject to the Father of spirits, and live?

Hebrews 13:17
Obey your leaders and submit to them, for they keep watch over your souls as those who will give an account. Let them do this with joy and not with grief, for this would be unprofitable for you.

James 4:7
Submit therefore to God Resist the devil and he will flee from you.

Luke 22:42
saying, "Father, if You are willing, remove this cup from Me; yet not My will, but Yours be done."

Matthew 26:39
And He went a little beyond them, and fell on His face and prayed, saying, "My Father, if it is possible, let this cup pass from Me; yet not as I will, but as You will."

Mark 14:36
And He was saying, "Abba! Father! All things are possible for You; remove this cup from Me; yet not what I will, but what You will."

John 5:19
Therefore Jesus answered and was saying to them, "Truly, truly, I say to you, the Son can do nothing of Himself, unless it is something He sees the Father doing; for whatever the Father does, these things the Son also does in like manner.

John 12:49-50
"For I did not speak on My own initiative, but the Father Himself who sent Me has given Me a commandment as to what to say and what to speak. "I know that His commandment is eternal life; therefore the things I speak, I speak just as the Father has told Me."

1 Corinthians 15:27-28
For HE HAS PUT ALL THINGS IN SUBJECTION UNDER HIS FEET But when He says, "All things are put in subjection," it is evident that He is excepted who put all things in subjection to Him. When all things are subjected to Him, then the Son Himself also will be subjected to the One who subjected all things to Him, so that God may be all in all.

Hebrews 5:7-8
In the days of His flesh, He offered up both prayers and supplications with loud crying and tears to the One able to save Him from death, and He was heard because of His piety. Although He was a Son, He learned obedience from the things which He suffered.

Ephesians 5:21
and be subject to one another in the fear of Christ.

Philippians 2:5-7
Have this attitude in yourselves which was also in Christ Jesus, who, although He existed in the form of God, did not regard equality with God a thing to be grasped, but emptied Himself, taking the form of a bond-servant, and being made in the likeness of men.

Ephesians 5:24
But as the church is subject to Christ, so also the wives ought to be to their husbands in everything.

Ephesians 1:22-23
And He put all things in subjection under His feet, and gave Him as head over all things to the church, which is His body, the fullness of Him who fills all in all.

Colossians 1:18
He is also head of the body, the church; and He is the beginning, the firstborn from the dead, so that He Himself will come to have first place in everything.

Joshua 1:7-8
"Only be strong and very courageous; be careful to do according to all the law which Moses My servant commanded you; do not turn from it to the right or to the left, so that you may have success wherever you go. "This book of the law shall not depart from your mouth, but you shall meditate on it day and night, so that you may be careful to do according to all that is written in it; for then you will make your way prosperous, and then you will have success.

Psalm 119:133
Establish my footsteps in Your word, And do not let any iniquity have dominion over me.

Colossians 3:15
Let the peace of Christ rule in your hearts, to which indeed you were called in one body; and be thankful.

James 1:22-25
But prove yourselves doers of the word, and not merely hearers who delude themselves. For if anyone is a hearer of the word and not a doer, he is like a man who looks at his natural face in a mirror; for once he has looked at himself and gone away, he has immediately forgotten what kind of person he was.

Revelation 22:18-19

I testify to everyone who hears the words of the prophecy of this book: if anyone adds to them, God will add to him the plagues which are written in this book; and if anyone takes away from the words of the book of this prophecy, God will take away his part from the tree of life and from the holy city, which are written in this book.

Romans 13:1

Every person is to be in subjection to the governing authorities For there is no authority except from God, and those which exist are established by God.

1 Corinthians 16:15-16

Now I urge you, brethren (you know the household of Stephanas, that they were the first fruits of Achaia, and that they have devoted themselves for ministry to the saints), that you also be in subjection to such men and to everyone who helps in the work and labors.

1 Thessalonians 5:12-13

But we request of you, brethren, that you appreciate those who diligently labor among you, and have charge over you in the Lord and give you instruction, and that you esteem them very highly in love because of their work. Live in peace with one another.

1 Corinthians 14:32

and the spirits of prophets are subject to prophets;

Matthew 22:21
They said to Him, "Caesar's." Then He said to them, "Then render to Caesar the things that are Caesar's; and to God the things that are God's."

Mark 12:17
And Jesus said to them, "Render to Caesar the things that are Caesar's, and to God the things that are God's." And they were amazed at Him.

Luke 20:25
And He said to them, "Then render to Caesar the things that are Caesar's, and to God the things that are God's."

Romans 13:2-7
Therefore whoever resists authority has opposed the ordinance of God; and they who have opposed will receive condemnation upon themselves. For rulers are not a cause of fear for good behavior, but for evil. Do you want to have no fear of authority? Do what is good and you will have praise from the same; for it is a minister of God to you for good. But if you do what is evil, be afraid; for it does not bear the sword for nothing; for it is a minister of God, an avenger who brings wrath on the one who practices evil. read more.

Titus 3:1
Remind them to be subject to rulers, to authorities, to be obedient, to be ready for every good deed,

1 Peter 2:13-14

Submit yourselves for the Lord's sake to every human institution, whether to a king as the one in authority, or to governors as sent by him for the punishment of evildoers and the praise of those who do right.

Ephesians 5:22-24

Wives, be subject to your own husbands, as to the Lord. For the husband is the head of the wife, as Christ also is the head of the church, He Himself being the Savior of the body. But as the church is subject to Christ, so also the wives ought to be to their husbands in everything.

Colossians 3:18

Wives, be subject to your husbands, as is fitting in the Lord.

Titus 2:4-5

so that they may encourage the young women to love their husbands, to love their children, to be sensible, pure, workers at home, kind, being subject to their own husbands, so that the word of God will not be dishonored.

1 Peter 3:1

In the same way, you wives, be submissive to your own husbands so that even if any of them are disobedient to the word, they may be won without a word by the behavior of their wives,

Exodus 20:12
"Honor your father and your mother, that your days may be prolonged in the land which the LORD your God gives you.

Galatians 4:2
but he is under guardians and managers until the date set by the father.

Colossians 3:20
Children, be obedient to your parents in all things, for this is well-pleasing to the Lord.

Ephesians 6:5-8
Slaves, be obedient to those who are your masters according to the flesh, with fear and trembling, in the sincerity of your heart, as to Christ; not by way of eyeservice, as men-pleasers, but as slaves of Christ, doing the will of God from the heart. With good will render service, as to the Lord, and not to men,

Colossians 3:22-24
Slaves, in all things obey those who are your masters on earth, not with external service, as those who merely please men, but with sincerity of heart, fearing the Lord. Whatever you do, do your work heartily, as for the Lord rather than for men, knowing that from the Lord you will receive the reward of the inheritance It is the Lord Christ whom you serve.

Titus 2:9-10

Urge bondslaves to be subject to their own masters in everything, to be well-pleasing, not argumentative, not pilfering, but showing all good faith so that they will adorn the doctrine of God our Savior in every respect.

1 Peter 2:18

Servants, be submissive to your masters with all respect, not only to those who are good and gentle, but also to those who are unreasonable.

Leviticus 19:32

'You shall rise up before the grayheaded and honor the aged, and you shall revere your God; I am the LORD.

Ephesians 5:25-33

Husbands, love your wives, just as Christ also loved the church and gave Himself up for her, so that He might sanctify her, having cleansed her by the washing of water with the word, that He might present to Himself the church in all her glory, having no spot or wrinkle or any such thing; but that she would be holy and blameless.

Ephesians 6:4

Fathers, do not provoke your children to anger, but bring them up in the discipline and instruction of the Lord.

1 Timothy 2:1-2

First of all, then, I urge that entreaties and prayers, petitions and thanksgivings, be made on behalf of all men, for kings and all who are in authority, so that we may lead a tranquil and quiet life in all godliness and dignity.

1 Peter 5:1-4

Therefore, I exhort the elders among you, as your fellow elder and witness of the sufferings of Christ, and a partaker also of the glory that is to be revealed, shepherd the flock of God among you, exercising oversight not under compulsion, but voluntarily, according to the will of God; and not for sordid gain, but with eagerness; nor yet as lording it over those allotted to your charge, but proving to be examples to the flock

TEMPER ˈtempər/

a person's state of mind seen in terms of their being angry or calm

I was once told, "He who angers you, controls you." The temperature of your TEMPER is critical. Are you mild mannered or more of the hot headed type? Losing your TEMPER puts you at the disadvantage of being able to adequately or eloquently get your point across. Once you reach a certain pitch of tone, one has either zoned out or amped up with you. It is difficult to come to a resolution in the midst of confusion.

Controlling your TEMPER allows you to analyze situations, be more aware of your surroundings and to see things more clearly.

No one can feel comfortable with someone who is easily angered and capable of losing their TEMPER at the drop of a hat. Too many lives are altered or even ended because TEMPERS flared, someone lost control and is now unable to rewind and reset for a redo. Today, be conscience of your attitude and make an effort to be in control of your TEMPER. Spread love through a gentle tone.

Be at ease, live in peace and control your TEMPER.

TEMPTATION tem(p)ˈtāSH(ə)n/

a desire to do something, especially something wrong or unwise.

"Don't give in!" TEMPTATIONS stem from that which is desired. The forbidden fruit in the Garden of Eden is one of the most referred to examples of TEMPTATION. With set rules and regulations we UNDERSTAND that there are boundaries we are expected not to cross.
The object that has your attention and may even be obtainable with little to no effort, but hold consequences unimaginable.
Making an effort to move towards a dangling trinket that has peeked your interest but does not have your name on it can pull you into a direction that may shift your life off course.
TEMPTATION comes in many forms: chocolate bars, shiny cars, a chance to be with stars or even to travel afar… Just remember with every action there comes a reaction and God is watching. Do not let the gifts of this temporary world control the forever dwelling place of your soul.

TRIALS ˈtrī(ə)l/

&

TRIBULATIONS tribyəˈlāSH(ə)n/

TRIALS- a formal examination of evidence before a judge
TRIBULATIONS – a cause of great trouble or suffering

As seeds are carefully trialed in different growing conditions, we must weather the storm in order to mature and reach our full potential. God has never promised us all sunshine as He knew it would also take some rain to nourish us. The TRIALS and TRIBULATIONS we are faced with builds our character as we blossom.
TRIALS are placed before us to test us. When you are at your lowest, just remember God makes no mistakes. Pray without ceasing within the scriptures as preperation for the tests that are coming your way.

THE LAND OF UN

We have all lived on a block in the land of UN. Some of us have relocated a time or two. You may have even occupied a space more than once. Let's take a stroll through The Land of Un and identify where we stand today.

UNhappy with the way things are going in your life? Feel as if the slump has lasted too long? Wrestling with the happenings surrounding you can cause for action. Are you willing to respond?

UNresolved issues of the past not allowing you to move forward? Reflect on the bearings of the wounds that are holding you captive. There is no way to stitch a wound that we continuously reopen. Identify the problem, learn from it and suture it with a fiber of love. Let the healing process begin.

UNappologetic about your faith. You should be steadfast in believing God has already worked it out.

UNeasy tokeep things the way they are? As our faith strengthens and our relationship grows with Christ, conviction will begin to weigh on your conscience. Knowing better, requires us to do better.

UNknown territories will test your ability to walk by faith and not by sight. Navigating through waters of depths that will lead us to trust God will hold us as we lean on Him and not our own compass. He will take us to places we have begun to comprehend as obtainable.

UNafraid for God has not given us the spirit of fear but of power and of love and of a sound mind. 2Timothy 1:7

UNavailable should be your mindset for circles of those you know are not heading in the direction your steps have been ordered to go.

UNcomfortable situations will require you to make a move. Growth begins where your faith meets your actions.

UNequipped is a soldier without a shield. Serving in the army of the Lord you must gear up wearing the armor of Christ daily.

UNdecided on which path to take? Pray and ask God to guide your steps. Let Him lead you to where He intends for you to be.

UNpredictable twists and turns in life can knock us off the path we planned on traveling. Knowing that our lives are evolving we must adjust the sails while at sea. Do not allow the movement to shake your faith but to strengthen it along the journey.

UNproductive in your goals? Being stagnant can add to your frustration. Sitting on a dream too long can become a nightmare. Be enthused about fulfilling your role in the kingdom. Be about your Father's business. *"As long as it is day, we must do the works of him who sent me. Night is coming, when no one can work."* John 9:4KJV

UNITY /ˈyoonədē/

the state of being one; oneness

The world we live in today is so divided we have difficulty attempting to find direction. Everyone is pushing and pulling and we find ourselves spinning wheels and going in circles. Where there is no UNITY we will continue parting ways. Meeting of the minds and standing firm on a solid foundation will grant us the opportunity to get many things accomplished. We begin to face adversities when we put aside the ability to agree to disagree when opinions differ.

The word states in Colossians 3:13-14 ….

13 Bear with each other and forgive one another if any of you has a grievance against someone. Forgive as the Lord forgave you. 14 And over all these virtues put on love, which binds them all together in perfect unity.

We may say "there is no perfect formula", but the Lord has made it clear in His teachings that we are to follow the guidelines and instructions. Do not attempt to say what you are not willing to show within your actions.

1 Corinthians 1:10
I appeal to you, brothers and sisters, in the name of our Lord Jesus Christ, that all of you agree with one another in what you say and that there be no divisions among you, but that you be perfectly united in mind and thought.

Being UNITED as one in the body of Christ, not allowing distractions to divide us by appearing to be the fork in the road we will lead nations to come together. It is up to us to carry out the vision of becoming one in the Lord. Grounding ourselves in the word, understanding the mission and accepting our role within the kingdom will create a UNITED force that is able to withstand the storm.

Ephesians 4:11-13
So Christ himself gave the apostles, the prophets, the evangelists, the pastors and teachers, 12 to equip his people for works of service, so that the body of Christ may be built up 13 until we all reach unity in the faith and in the knowledge of the Son of God and become mature, attaining to the whole measure of the fullness of Christ.

John 17:23
I in them and you in me—so that they may be brought to complete unity. Then the world will know that you sent me and have loved them even as you have loved me.

Psalm 133:1
How good and pleasant it is when God's people live together in unity!

1 Peter 3:8
Finally, all of you, be like-minded, be sympathetic, love one another, be compassionate and humble.

Romans 12:16
Live in harmony with one another. Do not be proud, but be willing to associate with people of low position. Do not be conceited.

Philippians 2:1
Therefore if you have any encouragement from being united with Christ, if any comfort from his love, if any common sharing in the Spirit, if any tenderness and compassion,

Ephesians 1:10
to be put into effect when the times reach their fulfillment—to bring unity to all things in heaven and on earth under Christ.

2 Chronicles 30:12
Also in Judah the hand of God was on the people to give them unity of mind to carry out what the king and his officials had ordered, following the word of the LORD.

Ephesians 2:14
For he himself is our peace, who has made the two groups one and has destroyed the barrier, the dividing wall of hostility,

Galatians 3:26-28
So in Christ Jesus you are all children of God through faith, for all of you who were baptized into Christ have clothed yourselves with Christ. There is neither Jew nor Gentile, neither slave nor free, nor is there male and female, for you are all one in Christ Jesus.

Ephesians 4:16

From him the whole body, joined and held together by every supporting ligament, grows and builds itself up in love, as each part does its work.

Romans 6:5

For if we have been united with him in a death like his, we will certainly also be united with him in a resurrection like his.

UPLIFT əp'lift/

elevate or stimulate (someone) morally or spiritually

UPLIFT the name of Christ. Let the words you speak today encourage those around you as you UPLIFT them through trying times. Look at the circumstances we are faced with as the perfect time to praise the name of the Lord knowing that He will UPLIFT those who exalt Him. Quit letting the devil whisper negative things in your ear to speak into your life or the life of those in your presence. Prepare yourself to elevate to heights that at one time may have frightened you. You shall be mounted with the wings of an eagle that you may soar.

In Isaiah 40:31 the word states:
But they that wait upon the Lord shall renew their strength; they shall mount up with wings as eagles, they shall run and not be weary, and they shall walk and not faint.

The world may be ever changing, but the word of the Lord stands true today and forevermore.

John 16:33
"I have told you these things, so that in me you may have peace. In this world you will have trouble. But take heart! I have overcome the world."

2 Timothy 1:7
For the Spirit God gave us does not make us timid, but gives us power, love and self-discipline.

Psalm 16:8

I keep my eyes always on the LORD. With him at my right hand, I will not be shaken.

Psalm 119:50
My comfort in my suffering is this: Your promise preserves my life.

Psalm 120:1
I call on the LORD in my distress, and he answers me.

UNDERSTANDING SEASONS

Ecclesiastes 3:1-8 KJV

1 There is a time for everything, and a season for every activity under the heavens:
2 a time to be born and a time to die, a time to plant and a time to uproot,
3 a time to kill and a time to heal, a time to tear down and a time to build,
4 a time to weep and a time to laugh, a time to mourn and time to dance,
5 a time to scatter stones and a time to gather them; a time to embrace and a time to refrain from embracing;
6 a time to search and a time to give up; a time to keep and a time to throw away;
7 a time to tear and a time to mend, a time to be silent and a time to speak;
8 a time to love and a time to hate; a time for war and a time for peace.

With every season, there comes change.
With every change there comes an adjustment.
With every adjustment there comes another level of sacrifice.
With every sacrifice there comes another reward.
With every reward there comes yet another testimony of how you conquered defeat.

The decisions you make today will place you a step closer to the destiny to be fulfilled by your desires.
Will you sell yourself short by giving in to a choice of instant gratification or stay on the course which may require long suffering… test your endurance or even your faith?

We live in such a microwave generation that we want everything at our fingertips… RIGHT NOW!
Don't be fooled into thinking that modern technology has given us the RIGHT NOW luxury…
Long before microwaves, cell phones, face time and there being an app for that…
My God gave His word of being a RIGHT NOW God.

Hebrews 11:1 KJV reads…
NOW faith is the substance of things hoped for… the evidence of things not seen…

NOW faith…. NOW faith…. NOW faith
Serving a right NOW God… the God who did it for Daniel in the lion's den is the same God that can work your miracle for you RIGHT NOW!

"UNDERSTANDING SEASONS"

Trust the process… better yet… pray and ask God to teach you to trust Him through the process.

Ecclessiastes 1:1
There is a time for everything, and a season for every activity under the heavens.

I'm here to tell you God has not forgotten about you in this season.
Those tears of pain… had their season. It's the season for tears of joy.
Those nights you walked up and down the halls worrying are over.
Give it to God and go to sleep.

Proverbs 3:24
When you lie down, you will not be afraid; when you lie down, your sleep will be sweet.

It's your season to rest and watch the fruit of your labor come to harvest.
The season of being last… you knew God wouldn't let it last….

It states in His word…

Matthew 20:16 KJV
So the last will be first, and the first will be last.

UNDERSTANDING SEASONS

Luke 20:43
Until I humble your enemies making them a footstool under your feet.

Fix your crown ... it is your season to birth visions... nurture generations and be the example, atmosphere adjusters and respect redeemers.

Before you begin UNDERSTANDING SEASONS...
You first have to understand who and WHO's you are...
   You are a child of God. The almighty King...

Revelation 22:13 KJV
I am the Alpha and the Omega, the First and the Last, the Beginning and the End.

He said you were created in His image... My God is great... it is your season to walk in greatness...
I encourage you to put one foot in front of the other and keep stepping until you step right into your dreams. Pray for guidance. Pray for wisdom...

Pray for UNDERSTANDING this SEASON......

LFS

VISION | ˌvɪʒən |
the faculty or state of being able to see

: the ability to think about or plan the future with imagination or wisdom

a mental image of what the future will or could be like : a socialist vision of society.

What do you want for your life? Your VISION will find victory when you learn to apply God's words to your everyday life.
VISIONS are given to us by God and our obedience to hinder unto His direction allows us to bring the VISION unto fruition. Why is VISION so important? It is tied to the outcome of your destiny. Where you see yourself is the direction you will travel. The inability to see yourself in certain standings will leave room for you to drift.
If we want happiness, blessings and prosperity, it is directly connected to our willingness to take heed unto God's orders. Submit nto our heavenly Father and sincerely ask Him to show where you are to be and to guide you in all areas of your life.

Proverbs 29:18
Where there is no vision, the people are unrestrained, But happy is he who keeps the law.

Seeing the turnaround in situations that others may have given up on or casted out, is the VISION that may breathe life and bring about the needed change. Having the

VISION does not end there.

It requires work to no end. When others do not see the purpose of the effort, you have to keep on keeping on as God has shown you what is.
Giving up on your VISION does not mean the VISION was a lie. It required another level of faith, sacrifice and endurance.
Do not stand still and allow your VISION to become a nightmare. Put in the work and believe that God trusted you with the ability to not only change things for yourself, but to bring about change for others.

Revelation 22:4
they will see His face, and His name will be on their foreheads.

1 Corinthians 13:12
For now we see in a mirror dimly, but then face to face; now I know in part, but then I will know fully just as I also have been fully known.

Psalm 13:3
Consider and answer me, O LORD my God; Enlighten my eyes, or I will sleep the sleep of death,

Ezekiel 12:22
"Son of man, what is this proverb you people have concerning the land of Israel, saying, 'The days are long and every vision fails'?

1 Samuel 3:1
Now the boy Samuel was ministering to the LORD before Eli And word from the LORD was rare in those days, visions were infrequent.

Daniel 10:7
Now I, Daniel, alone saw the vision, while the men who were with me did not see the vision; nevertheless, a great dread fell on them, and they ran away to hide themselves.

Genesis 46:2-4
God spoke to Israel in visions of the night and said, "Jacob, Jacob." And he said, "Here I am."

Genesis 15:1
After these things the word of the LORD came to Abram in a vision, saying, "Do not fear, Abram, I am a shield to you; Your reward shall be very great."

Genesis 40:5
Then the cupbearer and the baker for the king of Egypt, who were confined in jail, both had a dream the same night, each man with his own dream and each dream with its own interpretation.

Numbers 12:6
He said, "Hear now My words: If there is a prophet among you, I, the LORD, shall make Myself known to him in a vision I shall speak with him in a dream.

Psalm 31:22
As for me, I said in my alarm, "I am cut off from before Your eyes"; Nevertheless You heard the voice of my supplications When I cried to You.

Psalm 34:15
The eyes of the LORD are toward the righteous And His ears are open to their cry.

Psalm 139:16
Your eyes have seen my unformed substance; And in Your book were all written The days that were ordained for me, When as yet there was not one of them.

Zechariah 4:10
"For who has despised the day of small things? But these seven will be glad when they see the plumb line in the hand of Zerubbabel--these are the eyes of the LORD which range to and fro throughout the earth."

Genesis 6:5
Then the LORD saw that the wickedness of man was great on the earth, and that every intent of the thoughts of his heart was only evil continually.

1 Samuel 2:3
"Boast no more so very proudly, Do not let arrogance come out of your mouth; For the LORD is a God of knowledge, And with Him actions are weighed.

Proverbs 15:11
Sheol and Abaddon lie open before the LORD, How much more the hearts of men!

Jeremiah 20:12
Yet, O LORD of hosts, You who test the righteous, Who see the mind and the heart; Let me see Your vengeance on them; For to You I have set forth my cause.

Matthew 6:8
"So do not be like them; for your Father knows what you need before you ask Him.

Luke 16:15
And He said to them, "You are those who justify yourselves in the sight of men, but God knows your hearts; for that which is highly esteemed among men is detestable in the sight of God.

Hebrews 4:13
And there is no creature hidden from His sight, but all things are open and laid bare to the eyes of Him with whom we have to do.

1 John 3:20
in whatever our heart condemns us; for God is greater than our heart and knows all things.

Exodus 4:11
The LORD said to him, "Who has made man's mouth? Or who makes him mute or deaf, or seeing or blind? Is it not I, the LORD?

Psalm 146:8

The LORD opens the eyes of the blind; The LORD raises up those who are bowed down; The LORD loves the righteous;

Leviticus 26:16

I, in turn, will do this to you: I will appoint over you a sudden terror, consumption and fever that will waste away the eyes and cause the soul to pine away; also, you will sow your seed uselessly, for your enemies will eat it up.

VESSEL | |ˌvɛsəl|

a hollow container, esp. one used to hold liquid, such as a bowl or cask.

"Lord, use me as your VESSEL." Whisper those words with sincerity and ask the Lord to use you to glorify and magnify His name.
God desires us to humble ourselves, submitting to the word and being a VESSEL to use for His glory. Are you that VESSEL? Being the trusted instrument to carry the praise of the Almighty shows our level of commitment to our calling. Your ability to obey the instructions given in order to be that beacon of light the world needs to see during the darkest times. Ask the Lord to purge you of anything and everything that is not of Him in your life. Ask the Lord to bind and cast out any wrong spirit that is in your life distracting you from the work you have be assigned to do.
Ask the lord to have His way in your life and to lead you where you are most effective in spreading His word.
Are you ready to surrender yourself unto the Lord? Break me O Lord, melt me, fill me and use me for your glory.

2 Timothy 2:21
Therefore, if anyone cleanses himself from these things, he will be a vessel for honor, sanctified, useful to the Master, prepared for every good work.

Ezra 8:28
Then I said to them, "You are holy to the LORD, and the utensils are holy; and the silver and the gold are a freewill offering to the LORD God of your fathers.

Ezra 8:27
and 20 gold bowls worth 1,000 darics, and two utensils of fine shiny bronze, precious as gold.

Numbers 5:17
and the priest shall take holy water in an earthenware vessel; and he shall take some of the dust that is on the floor of the tabernacle and put it into the water.

Numbers 3:31
Now their duties involved the ark, the table, the lampstand, the altars, and the utensils of the sanctuary with which they minister, and the screen, and all the service concerning them;

1 Kings 7:45
and the pails and the shovels and the bowls; even all these utensils which Hiram made for King Solomon in the house of the LORD were of polished bronze.

1 Kings 8:4
They brought up the ark of the LORD and the tent of meeting and all the holy utensils, which were in the tent, and the priests and the Levites brought them up.

2 Kings 25:14
They took away the pots, the shovels, the snuffers, the spoons, and all the bronze vessels which were used in temple service.

2 Chronicles 36:18
All the articles of the house of God, great and small, and the treasures of the house of the LORD, and the treasures of the king and of his officers, he brought them all to Babylon.

Ezra 1:7
Also King Cyrus brought out the articles of the house of the LORD, which Nebuchadnezzar had carried away from Jerusalem and put in the house of his gods;

Jeremiah 28:3
'Within two years I am going to bring back to this place all the vessels of the LORD'S house, which Nebuchadnezzar king of Babylon took away from this place and carried to Babylon.

Daniel 1:2
The Lord gave Jehoiakim king of Judah into his hand, along with some of the vessels of the house of God; and he brought them to the land of Shinar, to the house of his god, and he brought the vessels into the treasury of his god.

Daniel 5:2

When Belshazzar tasted the wine, he gave orders to bring the gold and silver vessels which Nebuchadnezzar his father had taken out of the temple which was in Jerusalem, so that the king and his nobles, his wives and his concubines might drink from them.

VICTORY ˈvikt(ə)rē/

an act of defeating an enemy or opponent in a battle, game, or other competition.

The VICTORY is not ours, but it is the Lord's. Wear the full armor of the Lord. Know that there will never be a time that He shall leave you to fight a battle alone. Stand still, trust and believe that God will honor His word and protect you during your darkest hour. Look at the bigger picture and see that it was never a loss but a lesson to be learned. The true VICTORY comes when we give God all of the honor and praise in the midst of the turmoil. VICTORY is won long before we reach the finish line. It is only when you can say "Thank you Lord" in advance that we have become VICTORIOUS over the enemy. The enemy's job is to distract you and cloud your vision.
The road may get bumpy, we may feel the pressure building and at times the clouds may hang lower than we would like, but stay strong and know that the VICTORY is already won.

Proverbs 21:31

The horse is made ready for the day of battle, but victory rests with the LORD.

Deuteronomy 20:1-4

"When you go out to battle against your enemies and see horses and chariots and people more numerous than you, do not be afraid of them; for the LORD your God, who brought you up from the land of Egypt, is with you. "When you are approaching the battle, the priest shall come near and speak to the people. "He shall say to them, 'Hear, O Israel, you are approaching the battle against your enemies today. Do not be fainthearted. Do not be afraid, or panic, or tremble before them, read more.

2 Chronicles 20:15

and he said, "Listen, all Judah and the inhabitants of Jerusalem and King Jehoshaphat: thus says the LORD to you, 'Do not fear or be dismayed because of this great multitude, for the battle is not yours but God's.

Psalm 18:35

You have also given me the shield of Your salvation, And Your right hand upholds me; And Your gentleness makes me great.

1 Corinthians 15:57

but thanks be to God, who gives us the victory through our Lord Jesus Christ.

2 Corinthians 2:14

But thanks be to God, who always leads us in triumph in Christ, and manifests through us the sweet aroma of the knowledge of Him in every place.

Psalm 20:7-8

Some boast in chariots and some in horses, But we will boast in the name of the LORD, our God. They have bowed down and fallen, But we have risen and stood upright.

1 Samuel 17:45-47

Then David said to the Philistine, "You come to me with a sword, a spear, and a javelin, but I come to you in the name of the LORD of hosts, the God of the armies of Israel, whom you have taunted. "This day the LORD will deliver you up into my hands, and I will strike you down and remove your head from you. And I will give the dead bodies of the army of the Philistines this day to the birds of the sky and the wild beasts of the earth, that all the earth may know that there is a God in Israel, and that all this assembly may know that the LORD does not deliver by sword or by spear; for the battle is the LORD'S and He will give you into our hands."

Psalm 44:3-7

For by their own sword they did not possess the land, And their own arm did not save them, But Your right hand and Your arm and the light of Your presence, For You favored them. You are my King, O God; Command victories for Jacob. Through You we will push back our adversaries; Through Your name we will trample down those who rise up against us.

Psalm 60:11-12

O give us help against the adversary, For deliverance by man is in vain. Through God we shall do valiantly, And it is He who will tread down our adversaries.

Psalm 146:3
Do not trust in princes, In mortal man, in whom there is no salvation.

Proverbs 21:31
The horse is prepared for the day of battle, But victory belongs to the LORD.

Psalm 118:15
The sound of joyful shouting and salvation is in the tents of the righteous; The right hand of the LORD does valiantly.

Exodus 15:1
Then Moses and the sons of Israel sang this song to the LORD, and said, "I will sing to the LORD, for He is highly exalted; The horse and its rider He has hurled into the sea.

Psalm 21:1
O LORD, in Your strength the king will be glad, And in Your salvation how greatly he will rejoice!

1 Chronicles 22:13
"Then you will prosper, if you are careful to observe the statutes and the ordinances which the LORD commanded Moses concerning Israel Be strong and courageous, do not fear nor be dismayed.

Exodus 23:20-23
"Behold, I am going to send an angel before you to guard you along the way and to bring you into the place which I have prepared. "Be on your guard before him and obey his voice; do not be rebellious toward him, for he will not pardon your transgression, since My name is in him. "But if you truly obey his voice and do all that I say, then I will be an enemy to your enemies and an adversary to your adversaries.

Psalm 112:8
His heart is upheld, he will not fear, Until he looks with satisfaction on his adversaries.

Proverbs 2:7
He stores up sound wisdom for the upright; He is a shield to those who walk in integrity,

Numbers 14:41-43
But Moses said, "Why then are you transgressing the commandment of the LORD, when it will not succeed? "Do not go up, or you will be struck down before your enemies, for the LORD is not among you. "For the Amalekites and the Canaanites will be there in front of you, and you will fall by the sword, inasmuch as you have turned back from following the LORD. And the LORD will not be with you."

Deuteronomy 28:15
"But it shall come about, if you do not obey the LORD your God, to observe to do all His commandments and His statutes with which I charge you today, that all these curses will come upon you and

overtake you:

2 Chronicles 24:20
Then the Spirit of God came on Zechariah the son of Jehoiada the priest; and he stood above the people and said to them, "Thus God has said, 'Why do you transgress the commandments of the LORD and do not

1 Chronicles 11:4-9
Then David and all Israel went to Jerusalem (that is, Jebus); and the Jebusites, the inhabitants of the land, were there. The inhabitants of Jebus said to David, "You shall not enter here." Nevertheless David captured the stronghold of Zion (that is, the city of David). Now David had said, "Whoever strikes down a Jebusite first shall be chief and commander." Joab the son of Zeruiah went up first, so he became chief.

Genesis 50:20
"As for you, you meant evil against me, but God meant it for good in order to bring about this present result, to preserve many people alive.

Judges 16:24
When the people saw him, they praised their god, for they said, "Our god has given our enemy into our hands, Even the destroyer of our country, Who has slain many of us."

Romans 8:28
And we know that God causes all things to work together for good to those who love God, to those who are called according to His purpose.

Isaiah 41:25

"I have aroused one from the north, and he has come; From the rising of the sun he will call on My name; And he will come upon rulers as upon mortar, Even as the potter treads clay."

Isaiah 45:13

"I have aroused him in righteousness And I will make all his ways smooth; He will build My city and will let My exiles go free, Without any payment or reward," says the LORD of hosts.

Ezekiel 33:27-29

"Thus you shall say to them, 'Thus says the Lord GOD, "As I live, surely those who are in the waste places will fall by the sword, and whoever is in the open field I will give to the beasts to be devoured, and those who are in the strongholds and in the caves will die of pestilence. "I will make the land a desolation and a waste, and the pride of her power will cease; and the mountains of Israel will be desolate so that no one will pass through. "Then they will know that I am the LORD, when I make the land a desolation and a waste because of all their abominations which they have committed."'

Acts 2:36

"Therefore let all the house of Israel know for certain that God has made Him both Lord and Christ--this Jesus whom you crucified."

Acts 3:17-18

"And now, brethren, I know that you acted in ignorance, just as your rulers did also. "But the things which God announced beforehand by the mouth of all the prophets, that His Christ would suffer, He has thus fulfilled.

WILLINGNESS will·ing

Disposed or inclined; prepared

WILL you allow yourself to move out of your own way? Are you able to bend your determination of doing things your way and submit to following orders of another command?
A path of less resistance may not be as trying if we are entering the lanes prepared to give with another level of WILLINGESS. WILLING to admit others advice may be worth taking. WILLING to admit that we were wrong. Learning from others travels through this journey can help us navigate if we are WILLING to pay attention. Letting past occurrences build a fort of fear in your heart can prevent you from entering a chapter of warmth and growth that you deserve.
We only truly benefit from the past once we decide to respect the lessons it taught and we become WILLING to move forward with a different perspective because of it. Today I challenge you to balance your level of WILLINGNESS. Are you WILLING to release of the toxins in your life that you know are causing you harm? Are you WILLING to go the extra mile in order to succeed? How WILLING are you to submit fully to the WILL of God? Do not let life pass you by because you were not WILLING to try.

2 Corinthians 8:12KJV
For if there be first a willing mind, it is accepted according to that a man hath, and not according to that he hath not.

WITNESS ˈwitnəs/
evidence; proof.

Every day we WITNESS the greatness of the Lord.
His grace and mercy keeps us and covers us throughout
any danger, hurt or harm that the devil sends our way.
We WITNESS the promises kept as the sun rise in the East
and sets in the West. We WITNESS the stars shining in the
moonlit sky and know that it is God's design we are
admiring. We WITNESS these things and are expected to
be a WITNESS to others of the goodness of the Lord.
Once we see the evidence of God's word standing true, we
should begin to see things differently.
A different perspective on what may appear as natural
happenstance to the human eye. Things that may have been
a bland background in our everyday lives takes on a whole
new meaning as we zoom in through our spiritual lens.
After seeing all of the wonders God has worked in my life,
I would not want to let the rocks cry out on my behalf.
Stand on the solid foundation that has been built on the
promises of the Lord.
Be a WITNESS of His magnificence.

Luke 19:40
"I tell you," he replied, "if they keep quiet, the stones will cry out."

Matthew 4:19
Jesus called out to them, "Come, follow me, and I will show you how to fish for people!"

Isaiah 55:11
so is my word that goes out from my mouth: It will not return to me empty, but will accomplish what I desire and achieve the purpose for which I sent it.

Matthew 24:14
And this gospel of the kingdom will be proclaimed throughout the whole world as a testimony to all nations, and then the end will come.

1 Peter 3:15
Instead, you must worship Christ as Lord of your life. And if someone asks about your Christian hope, always be ready to explain it.

Mark 16:15-16
And he said unto them, Go ye into all the world, and preach the gospel to every creature. He that believeth and is baptized shall be saved; but he that believeth not shall be damned.

Romans 10:15
And how can anyone preach unless they are sent? As it is written: "How beautiful are the feet of those who bring good news!"

Matthew 9:37-38
Then he said to his disciples, "The harvest is plentiful but the workers are few. Ask the Lord of the harvest, therefore, to send out workers into his harvest field."

Matthew 5:16
In the same way, let your light shine before others, that they may see your good deeds and glorify your Father in heaven.

Romans 1:16
For I am not ashamed of this Good News about Christ. It is the power of God at work, saving everyone who believes—the Jew first and also the Gentile

2 Timothy 1:8
So do not be ashamed of the testimony about our Lord or of me his prisoner. Rather, join with me in suffering for the gospel, by the power of God.

Luke 12:12
For the Holy Ghost shall teach you in the same hour what ye ought to say.

Matthew 10:20
for it will not be you speaking, but the Spirit of your Father speaking through you.

Romans 8:26
Likewise the Spirit helps us in our weakness. For we do not know what to pray for as we ought, but the Spirit himself intercedes for us with groanings too deep for words.

WORDS wərd/

a single distinct meaningful element of speech or writing, used with others

WORDS are powerful.
It may not always be what you say, but how you say it stands to be true… but the WORDS which are spoken carries weight. It was WORDS that God spoke the world into existence.

Genesis 1:3
And God said, Let there be light: and there was light.

Genesis 1:6
And God said, Let there be a firmament in the midst of the waters, and let it divide the waters from the waters.

Genesis 1:9
And God said, Let the waters under the heaven be gathered together unto one place, and let the dry land appear: and it was so.

Genesis 1:11
And God said, Let the earth bring forth grass, the herb yielding seed, and the fruit tree yielding fruit after his kind, whose seed is in itself, upon the earth: and it was so.

Genesis 1:14
And God said, Let there be lights in the firmament of the heaven to divide the day from the night; and let them be for signs, and for seasons, and for days, and years:

Genesis 1:20
And God said, Let the waters bring forth abundantly the moving creature that hath life, and fowl that may fly above the earth in the open firmament of heaven.

Genesis 1:24
And God said, Let the earth bring forth the living creature after his kind, cattle, and creeping thing, and beast of the earth after his kind: and it was so.

Genesis 1:26
And God said, Let us make man in our image, after our likeness: and let them have dominion over the fish of the sea, and over the fowl of the air, and over the cattle, and over all the earth, and over every creeping thing that creepeth upon the earth.

Genesis 1:29
And God said, Behold, I have given you every herb bearing seed, which is upon the face of all the earth, and every tree, in which is the fruit of a tree yielding seed: to you it shall be for meat.

WORDS are powerful. Speaking things into existence and believing that the WORDS from our lips are reaching God's ears can bring us to fill and rule places and spaces greater than we ever expected.

You can either speak life or death, the choice is yours. Are the WORDS you chose in line with the WORD you say you believe in and live by?

I challenge you to observe the tone of your WORDS.
I challenge you to observe your selection of WORDS.
I challenge you to justify the WORDS you use in your daily dialogue as they align with God's WORD.

WORDS are powerful. God gave us the example as He spoke to us in the beginning and it was so.

XRAY ˈeks ˌrā/

an electromagnetic wave of high energy and very short wavelength, which is able to pass through many materials opaque to light.

Today, take a closer look at what is right in front of you through a different light.
The fracture is there, but may not make itself visible to the naked eye. The pain alerts you that something below the surface is unsettling and needs immediate attention, but you cannot see the severity of the problem until you look at the canvas through a different light.
Our light through our heavenly Father allows us to examine situations that are causing us grief, pain and unbearable sorrow once we are willing to view the broken surface through X-RAY vision. The light of the Lord will be all that we need to see beyond the circumstances that are cloudy at first sight.

1 Corinthians 13:12
For now we see in a mirror dimly, but then face to face. Now I know in part; then I shall know fully, even as I have been fully known.

As we strengthen our relationship with Christ, the vision will become clearer than ever. As we begin to mature as Christians we will be able to dig deeper, identify the cracked surface and heal with the guidance of our Savior.

YOU yoo,yə/

used to refer to the person or people that the speaker is addressing

YOU are the child of a King.
YOU have been promised unconditional love that will be there even through the most trying times.
YOU have the ability to change the world.
YOU will go through challenges that will build strength, endurance and faith.
YOU will nurture generations to come.
YOU will be the deciding factor of your journey's route.
YOU have the choice to follow Christ or to join forces with the devil's workshop.
YOU are responsible for your actions.
YOU will be held accountable for the things you say and do.
YOU are beautifully and wonderfully made.
YOU are destined for greatness.
YOU are more than a conqueror.
YOU are a warrior, do not let circumstances encourage the spirit of a worrier.
YOU are a leader.
YOU are to shine your light so bright that others will be drawn to Christ.
YOU are gifted… tap into your source and magnify the Lord.
YOU know that now is the time to quit procrastinating.

It all starts with YOU.

YOUTH yooTH/

the period between childhood and adult age.

YOUTH today are some of the most innovative thinkers. Although we live in a world where so many thing are convenient through technology, our YOUTH continuously bridge the gap between concept and reality.
YOUTH understand that if you truly want something, there is a way to make it happen. They are looking at life through a vision of faith.
They believe that possibilities are limitless and no is not an option when God has granted them a vision of their destiny.
Our YOUTH begin to work the process of elimination of people and things that may stand between them and their purpose. As we grow through life, we encounter situations that blots our enthusiasm, dampens our spirits and may even halt our progress.
Growing through life with a YOUTHFUL outlook will help us to realize that we are stronger than we thought we were.
We can accomplish all goals we set and more, once we apply ourselves and do so willingly and with a YOUTHFUL spirit. It is not meant for us to grow weary and faint as the Lord has promised to renew and restore. Aim higher and walk through the walls of adversity knowing that God has already made good on His words promised to you.

ZOOM \'züm\
to adjust the lens of a camera to adjust its lens so that the image seems to be bigger and closer

ZOOM in and take a closer look at whatever it is that your heart truly desires. Is your focus on the things that are aligned with God's promises?
Once you have ZOOMED in, taking a closer look at the desires of your heart and the intent of your actions, ask yourself, "Is this something that is pleasing unto God's sight? Is this worthy of my efforts in hopes of being helpful to the value of humanity?"

A closer view of peace, love and charity will allow us to see where it is lacking.
A closer view of a hurting world will point out isolated situations with the same missing ingredients of peace, love and charity.

ZOOM into the cause of the hurt inflicting pain to others.
ZOOM into the cure of mending broken hearts and restoring them with a bond of hope.
So many have lost their way because the light has grown dim and no one has ZOOMED in to see the issue.
Take a closer look starting with self and pray for guidance to help change things for the better while spreading encouragement to others to do the same.

ZONE zōn/

an area or stretch of land having a particular characteristic, purpose, or use, or subject to particular restrictions.

Get out of your comfort ZONE and begin to activate your faith. Staying where you are content will not allow you to enter the next chapter of greatness that has already been preordained. The outcome for the course of actions you will experience once you open your mind will elevate you to levels beyond what is considered normal. Trust in the Lord and acknowledge Him in all of your ways.
Let Him guide you and know that He will never leave nor forsake you. When you roam pass the line of confinement where your ZONE is being stretched, thank God in advance for the preparation of elevation.
Ask Him to always be the voice of reason through every season.

Ask, "A – Z, Lord, Let It Define Me."

NOTES

ABOUT THE AUTHOR

LaTangela Sherman is recognized as the voice of her generation and leader in her community. She has etched her mark and expanded her brand as the go to in order to get it done effectively. With twenty years of experience in media as an On-Air Personality and Production Director she has been awarded Women In Media's Personality of the Year; Ambassador of the Year for the American Heart/Stroke Association; Champion Recruiter for City Year and The Voice of Tomorrow for Chevy and Essence Music Festival. "Opening the lines of communication, finding your voice and giving back will enhance the world we live in, one community at a time."
Other publications from LaTangela Sherman:

"Soul Inspirations" and "You Were Born A Brand"

www.430Status.com

www.ingramcontent.com/pod-product-compliance
Lightning Source LLC
Chambersburg PA
CBHW070645160426
43194CB00009B/1584